HBR'S 10 MUST READS

For
**Mid-Level
Managers**

The Sky is
the limit
- Rockwood
Industries

D1569034

The sky is
the limit
- Rockwood
Zachary

HBR's 10 Must Reads series is the definitive collection of ideas and best practices for aspiring and experienced leaders alike. These books offer essential reading selected from the pages of *Harvard Business Review* on topics critical to the success of every manager.

Titles include:

HBR's 10 Must Reads 2015
HBR's 10 Must Reads 2016
HBR's 10 Must Reads 2017
HBR's 10 Must Reads 2018
HBR's 10 Must Reads 2019
HBR's 10 Must Reads 2020
HBR's 10 Must Reads 2021
HBR's 10 Must Reads 2022
HBR's 10 Must Reads 2023
HBR's 10 Must Reads 2024
HBR's 10 Must Reads for CEOs
HBR's 10 Must Reads for Executive Teams
HBR's 10 Must Reads for Mid-Level Managers
HBR's 10 Must Reads for New Managers
HBR's 10 Must Reads on AI
HBR's 10 Must Reads on AI, Analytics, and the New Machine Age
HBR's 10 Must Reads on Boards
HBR's 10 Must Reads on Building a Great Culture
HBR's 10 Must Reads on Business Model Innovation
HBR's 10 Must Reads on Career Resilience
HBR's 10 Must Reads on Change Management (Volumes 1 and 2)
HBR's 10 Must Reads on Collaboration
HBR's 10 Must Reads on Communication (Volumes 1 and 2)
HBR's 10 Must Reads on Creativity
HBR's 10 Must Reads on Design Thinking
HBR's 10 Must Reads on Diversity
HBR's 10 Must Reads on Emotional Intelligence

HBR's 10 Must Reads on Entrepreneurship and Startups
HBR's 10 Must Reads on High Performance
HBR's 10 Must Reads on Innovation
HBR's 10 Must Reads on Leadership (Volumes 1 and 2)
HBR's 10 Must Reads on Leadership for Healthcare
HBR's 10 Must Reads on Leadership Lessons from Sports
HBR's 10 Must Reads on Leading Digital Transformation
HBR's 10 Must Reads on Lifelong Learning
HBR's 10 Must Reads on Making Smart Decisions
HBR's 10 Must Reads on Managing Across Cultures
HBR's 10 Must Reads on Managing in a Downturn, Expanded
    Edition
HBR's 10 Must Reads on Managing People (Volumes 1 and 2)
HBR's 10 Must Reads on Managing Risk
HBR's 10 Must Reads on Managing Yourself (Volumes 1 and 2)
HBR's 10 Must Reads on Mental Toughness
HBR's 10 Must Reads on Negotiation
HBR's 10 Must Reads on Nonprofits and the Social Sectors
HBR's 10 Must Reads on Organizational Resilience
HBR's 10 Must Reads on Performance Management
HBR's 10 Must Reads on Platforms and Ecosystems
HBR's 10 Must Reads on Public Speaking and Presenting
HBR's 10 Must Reads on Reinventing HR
HBR's 10 Must Reads on Sales
HBR's 10 Must Reads on Strategic Marketing
HBR's 10 Must Reads on Strategy (Volumes 1 and 2)
HBR's 10 Must Reads on Strategy for Healthcare
HBR's 10 Must Reads on Talent
HBR's 10 Must Reads on Teams
HBR's 10 Must Reads on Trust
HBR's 10 Must Reads on Women and Leadership
HBR's 10 Must Reads: The Essentials

For
Mid-Level
Managers

HARVARD BUSINESS REVIEW PRESS
Boston, Massachusetts

Library of Congress Cataloging-in-Publication Data

Names: Harvard Business Review Press, issuing body.
Title: HBR's 10 must reads for mid-level managers.
Other titles: Harvard Business Rreview's ten must reads for mid-level managers. | HBR's 10 must reads (Series)
Description: Boston, Massachusetts : Harvard Business Review Press, [2023] | Series: HBR's 10 must reads | Includes index.
Identifiers: LCCN 2023005856 (print) | LCCN 2023005857 (ebook) | ISBN 9781647824945 (paperback) | ISBN 9781647824952 (epub)
Subjects: LCSH: Middle managers. | Industrial management. | Success in business.
Classification: LCC HD38.24 .H37 2023 (print) | LCC HD38.24 (ebook) | DDC 658.4/3--dc23/eng/20230503
LC record available at https://lccn.loc.gov/2023005856
LC ebook record available at https://lccn.loc.gov/2023005857

ISBN: 978-1-64782-494-5
eISBN: 978-1-64782-495-2

The paper used in this publication meets the requirements of the American National Standard for Permanence of Paper for Publications and Documents in Libraries and Archives Z39.48-1992.

Contents

HBR'S 10 MUST READS

For
**Mid-Level
Managers**

Managers Can't Do It All

by Diane Gherson and Lynda Gratton

JENNIFER STARES AT HER UPWARD-FEEDBACK REPORT and wonders how she got to this point. How could a veteran like her, someone who was once celebrated as manager of the year, receive such negative ratings? She used to enjoy her role, but now everything feels out of control. Her job has been reshaped so constantly—by sweeping process reengineering, digitization, and agile initiatives, and most recently by remote work—that she always feels at least one step behind.

The amount of change that has taken place in just the past few years is overwhelming. The management layer above her was eliminated, which doubled the size of her team, and almost half the people on it are now working on cross-division projects led by *other* managers. She and her team used to meet in her office for progress reviews, but now she has no office, and if she wants to know how her people are doing, she has to join their stand-ups, which makes her feel like an onlooker rather than their boss. She no longer feels in touch with how everybody is doing, and yet she has the same set of personnel responsibilities as before: providing performance feedback, making salary adjustments, hiring and firing, engaging in career discussions.

Not only that, but she's being asked to take on even more. Because her company is rapidly digitizing, for example, she's responsible for upgrading her staff's technical skills. This makes her uncomfortable because it feels threatening to many of her team members. When she talks with them about it, she's expected to demonstrate endless amounts of empathy—something that has never been her strong suit. She's supposed to seek out diverse talent and create a climate of psychological safety while simultaneously downsizing the unit. She understands why all these things are important, but they're not what she signed up for when she became a manager, and she's just not sure that she has the emotional energy to handle them.

What happened to the stable, well-defined job that she was so good at for so long? What happened to the power and status that used to come with that job? Is *she* the problem? Is she simply no longer able to keep up with the demands of the evolving workplace? Is she now part of the "frozen middle"—the much-maligned layer of management that obstructs change rather than enables it?

Jennifer—a composite of several real people we have met in our work—has no answers to these questions. All she knows is that she's frustrated, unhappy, and overwhelmed.

As are managers everywhere.

One of us, Lynda, is an academic researcher and consultant to corporations, and the other, Diane, was until her recent retirement the chief human resources officer at IBM (in which she still owns stock). In those roles we have closely observed the changing job of the manager, and we can report that a crisis is looming.

The signs are everywhere. In 2021, when we asked executives from 60 companies around the world how their managers were doing, we got unanimous reports of frustration and exhaustion. Similarly, when the research firm Gartner asked 75 HR leaders from companies worldwide how their managers were faring, 68% reported that they were overwhelmed. Nonetheless, according to Gartner, only 14% of those companies had taken steps to help alleviate their managers' burdens.

The problem isn't hard to diagnose. The traditional role of the manager evolved in the hierarchical workplaces of the industrial age, but in our fluid, flatter, postindustrial age that role is beginning to look archaic.

The irony is that we actually need great people leaders more than ever. Microsoft has found, for example, that when managers help

Idea in Brief

The Problem

Managers are the lifeblood of organizations. In recent decades, as the workplace has changed, they've been asked to take on new responsibilities and demonstrate new skills—and are struggling to cope. This threatens productivity, employee well-being, and brand reputation.

The New Reality

Change has come along three dimensions: power (managers have to think about making teams successful, not being served by them); skills (they're expected to coach performance, not oversee tasks); and structure (they have to lead in more-fluid environments).

The Way Forward

We need to do everything we can to help managers adapt. The three companies featured in this article have deliberately—and successfully—transformed the role of manager so that it better meets the demands of 21st-century work.

---

teams prioritize, nurture their culture, and support work/life balance, employees feel more connected and are more positive about their work. The consulting firm O.C. Tanner has likewise found that weekly one-to-ones with managers during uncertain times lead to a 54% increase in engagement, a 31% increase in productivity, a 15% decrease in burnout, and a 16% decrease in depression among employees. Meanwhile, according to McKinsey, having good relationships with their managers is the top factor in employees' job satisfaction, which in turn is the second-most-important determinant of their overall well-being.

Conversely, bad managers can significantly hurt retention and engagement: Seventy-five percent of the participants in the McKinsey survey reported that the most stressful aspect of their jobs was their immediate boss. As the saying goes, people join companies and leave their managers.

Something is clearly broken. If managers remain essential but their traditional role has become obsolete, then it's obviously time for a change.

In this article we'll make the case for redefining and even splitting the role rather than simply continuing to let it evolve, which is a potentially costly and disastrous course of action. But first let's

3

briefly take stock of the waves of innovation that have brought us to this crisis point.

Four Defining Business Movements

The first wave, *process reengineering,* began in about 1990 and lasted until the early 2000s. It focused on eliminating bureaucracy and boosting operational efficiencies. With the help of consulting firms, which developed practices around this kind of work, companies globalized and outsourced their processes, flattened their hierarchies, and in many cases put their remaining managers in "player-coach" roles that required them to take on workers' tasks. These changes reduced costs, but they also made life a lot harder for managers. They now had wider responsibilities and significantly larger teams to supervise and were also expected to dedicate themselves personally to projects and customers.

The next wave of innovation, *digitization,* arrived in about 2010. Promisingly, it democratized access to both information and people, but in doing so it undermined traditional sources of managerial power. CEOs and other senior leaders could now communicate directly with their entire workforces, sharing strategies, priorities, and important updates and responding to concerns. No longer a necessary part of the information loop, managers began to feel a loss of power, control, and status.

Then came the *agile movement* and its process changes, which companies began to adopt in the mid to late 2010s. It aimed to shorten timelines and turbocharge innovation by using internal marketplaces across whole organizations to match skills to work and to rapidly assemble project teams on an as-needed basis. As a result, managers started to lose touch with their reports, who now spent much of their time under the rotating supervision of the project managers they were temporarily assigned to. And because candidates could be matched to openings online, managers lost the power and authority involved with brokering career opportunities for their people.

Finally, a fourth wave arrived in 2020 with the pandemic, when companies and employees were forced to embrace the possibilities of *flexible work*. This was a watershed moment. It dramatically altered how and where work was done. Once employees were no longer tied to a physical workplace, managers lost the close control that they used to have over employees' performance and behavior—and employees began to realize that they could tap a greater range of job options, far beyond commuting distance from their homes. These changes were liberating, but they placed even more of a burden on managers—who now were also expected to cultivate empathetic relationships that would allow them to engage and retain the people they supervised. (See the sidebar "Vertical Code-Switching Is Exhausting.")

These waves of innovation have changed the role of the manager along three dimensions: *power*, *skills*, and *structure*. In a power shift, managers have to think about making teams successful, not being served by them. In a skills shift, they're expected to coach performance, not oversee tasks; and in a structural shift, they have to lead in more-fluid environments. (See the exhibit "From manager to people leader.")

These changes have empowered employees, which of course is a good thing. But they've also altered how managers drive productivity. Organizations are starting to recognize this. When we asked the executives in our 60-company survey to list the most important areas that managers need to focus on today, their top answers were coaching, communication, and employee well-being.

New Models of Management

Some organizations have taken deliberate steps to reimagine the role of the manager. Let's take a look at transformative shifts that have been made at three very different companies in banking, tech, and telecommunications.

Building new skills at scale

Most companies think of their top leaders as the people who make change happen—and are willing to spend millions on their development as a result. The layers of management below the top, the theory

5

Vertical Code-Switching Is Exhausting

by Eric M. Anicich and Jacob B. Hirsh

MIDDLE MANAGERS are expected to play very different roles when moving from one interaction to the next, alternating between relatively high- and relatively low-power interaction styles. By virtue of their structural positions, they are simultaneously the "victims and the carriers of change" within an organization, receiving strategy prescriptions from their bosses above and having to implement those strategies with the people who work below them.[a] As a result, middle managers often find themselves stuck in between various stakeholder groups, which can produce relentless and conflicting demands.

According to Arizona State's Blake Ashforth and colleagues, these types of micro role transitions in the workplace can produce exactly the kind of role conflict that we propose middle managers are disproportionately likely to experience. In many cases, the norms and expectations associated with being a leader (for example, assertiveness) are incompatible with the norms and expectations associated with being a subordinate (for example, deference). This becomes problematic when one is called upon to play both roles at work, because humans are notoriously inefficient when it comes to task switching, as evidenced, for example, by research showing mood spillover effects from work to home and vice versa.[b] Simply put, it is psychologically challenging to disengage from a task that requires one mindset and engage in another task that requires a very different mindset.

This vertical code-switching, as we call it, can take a toll, according to a wide body of research. On the emotional side, conflicting roles lead to increased

goes, are frozen in place and will resist change. But the executives at Standard Chartered—a retail bank, headquartered in London, with more than 750 branches in 50-plus countries—recently chose to think differently. Their 14,000 middle managers, they decided, would play a central role in the bank's growth.

Rather than wholly redesigning the job, the executive team began with some basic steps: changing the role's title, creating an accreditation process, and strengthening the sense of a managerial community. Managers became "people leaders," an acknowledgment of how important the human connection was in their work. Meanwhile, the new accreditation process evaluated future-focused capabilities such as driving growth, building trust, aligning teams, and making feelings of stress and anxiety, reflecting the tension between incompatible social expectations. Physically, the high stress levels that accompany such conflicts are risk factors for a large number of health problems, from hypertension to heart disease. As if that weren't enough, conflicting roles can disrupt cognitive performance and the ability to focus on a task without getting distracted. In a large-scale epidemiological study involving survey responses from 21,859 full-time employees across a wide range of industries, for instance, researchers from Columbia University and the University of Toronto observed that employees in mid-level organizational positions had higher rates of depression and anxiety than employees who occupied positions nearer either end of the hierarchy, findings that can be added to the long list of reasons why middle managers are so unhappy.[c]

a. Antonio Giangreco and Riccardo Peccei, "The Nature and Antecedents of Middle Manager Resistance to Change: Evidence from an Italian Context," *The International Journal of Human Resource Management* 16, no. 10 (2005): 1812–1829, https://doi.org/10.1080/09585190500298404.

b. Kevin J. Williams and George M. Alliger, "Role Stressors, Mood Spillover, and Perceptions of Work-Family Conflict in Employed Parents," *Academy of Management Journal* 37, no. 4 (1994): 837–868, https://doi.org/10.5465/256602.

c. Seth J. Prins, Lisa M. Bates, Katherine M. Keyes, and Carles Muntaner, "Anxious? Depressed? You Might Be Suffering from Capitalism: Contradictory Class Locations and the Prevalence of Depression and Anxiety in the USA," *Sociology of Health & Illness* 37, no. 8 (2015): 1352–1372, https://doi.org/10.1111/1467-9566.12315.

Adapted from "Why Being a Middle Manager Is So Exhausting," Ascend, on hbr.org, March 22, 2017 (product #H03JR2).

bold decisions. And the executive team worked to strengthen community by applying the local experiences of people leaders to problems across the whole company. For example, when in the course of filling 10 positions, one cohort of people leaders failed to hire anybody from an underrepresented group, the executive team didn't single the group out for criticism but instead seized the opportunity to ask the whole community, "How can we support you in making your teams more diverse?"

Next the executive team decided to focus on coaching, which has today become a crucial management skill. (See "The Leader as Coach," by Herminia Ibarra and Anne Scoular, later in this volume.) Coaching, in fact, plays a key role in each of the three shifts we

From manager to people leader

Three fundamental shifts in the role of managers today

A power shift: from "me" to "we"

My team makes me successful.	→	I'm here to make my team successful.
I'm rewarded for achieving business goals.	→	I'm also rewarded for improving team engagement, inclusion, and skills relevancy.
I control how people move beyond my unit.	→	I scout for talent and help my team move fluidly to wider opportunities.

A skills shift: from task overseer to performance coach

I oversee work.	→	I track outcomes.
I assess team members against expectations.	→	I coach them to achieve their potential and invite their feedback on my management.
I provide work direction and share information from above.	→	I supply inspiration, sensemaking, and emotional support.

A structural shift: from static and physical to fluid and digital

I manage an intact team of people in fixed jobs in a physical workplace.	→	My team is fluid, and the workplace is digital.
I set goals and make assessments annually.	→	I provide ongoing guidance on priorities and performance feedback.
I hold an annual career discussion focused on the next promotion.	→	I'm always retraining my team and providing career coaching.

described earlier: When managers coach they're making a power shift by moving from instruction to support and guidance; a skills shift by moving from the oversight of work to the continual giving of feedback; and a structural shift by engaging with their people in a way that's dynamic and constant rather than static and episodic.

Standard Chartered had been working for decades on developing its top leaders into coaches. But now the challenge was scaling that effort up to 14,000 people leaders. The bank did this through a variety of initiatives—by using an AI-based coaching platform, for example, and by developing peer-to-peer and team coaching across all its markets in Africa, the Middle East, and Asia. It also launched a pilot project in which it offered to help people leaders pay for formal training and accreditation as coaches (by outside organizations approved by the global governing body for coaching). Those who accepted were expected to coach other employees; the goal was building what Tanuj Kapilashrami, the bank's head of human resources, describes as "a deep coaching culture." So many participants reported a boost in skills and confidence that the bank organized further rounds of training and accreditation, each of which was oversubscribed, with hundreds of people taking part around the world.

Rewiring processes and systems

In 2013, as IBM's new chief human resources officer, Diane realized that to support the massive transformation that had been launched by then-CEO Ginni Rometty, the company needed a different kind of manager. IBM was changing 50% of its product portfolio over the next five years, moving into several growth businesses (among them the cloud, AI, cybersecurity, and blockchain), and migrating from software licensing to software as a service. At a worldwide town hall, Rometty announced that all employees would be required not only to develop new skills but also to learn to work differently. The company would build a culture optimized for innovation and speed—and needed its managers to lead retraining efforts, adapt their management styles to agile work methods, and get all employees engaged in the journey.

That meant doing three things: freeing managers up for additional responsibilities by digitally transforming their work; equipping them with new skills; and holding them accountable through a metrics-driven performance-development system. Their most important goal was employee engagement: Managers account for 70% of the variance in that metric.

The HR function deployed AI to eliminate administrative work, such as approving expense reports or transferring employees to a new unit. Personalized digital learning was introduced so that managers could access support on their mobile phones—for, say, just-in-time guidance on preparing for difficult conversations. New AI-driven programs also helped managers make better people decisions and spot issues like attrition risk. An AI-driven adviser has made it easier for managers to determine salary increases: It considers not only performance and market pay gaps but also internal data on employee turnover by skills, the current external demand for each employee's skills (scraped from competitor job postings), and the future demand.

Now when managers have salary conversations with employees, they can confidently share the rationale for their decisions, help team members understand the demand for their skills, and, most important, focus on supporting them as they build market-relevant capabilities and accelerate their career growth.

Like Standard Chartered, IBM also introduced an accreditation for managers, built on a new training curriculum. The impact has been significant: Managers who have obtained this accreditation are scoring five points higher today on employee engagement than those who have not.

In addition, IBM requires managers to get "licenses" in key activities by undergoing an in-house certification program. Licenses to hire, for example, are designed to ensure that managers select candidates in an objective and unbiased way, provide them with a well-designed experience, and ultimately make hires of high quality. The impact has been significant here too: Employees hired by licensed managers are 7% more likely to exceed expectations at six months and 45% less likely to leave the company within their first year than other hires are. Those numbers mean a lot in a company that makes more than 50,000 hires a year.

One major shift is the deliberate change from performance management to performance development. Not just about business results, the new system reflects the mindset and skills needed to manage in the modern workplace.

Feedback is at its core. Team members are asked whether their managers create an environment that encourages candid communication. Do they provide frequent and meaningful feedback? Do they help in the development of market-relevant skills? Are they effective career coaches? At the same time, HR gathers metrics on diversity and inclusion, regretted attrition, and skills development. The company then combines those metrics with its survey data and feeds the results into its Manager Success Index—a dashboard that allows managers to understand how well they're meeting expectations and to identify needs for both learning and "unlearning." Managers are invited to training programs on the basis of their specific development needs. Investing in these programs pays off: People who have completed at least one course in the past two years are 20% less likely to be in the bottom decile of the Manager Success Index, whereas those who have taken no leadership development courses are much more likely to be there.

IBM takes this idea seriously. Managers who do not demonstrate growth behaviors and who consistently underperform get moved out of managerial positions. The message to the company's managers is clear: Times have changed, and you must too. Your ongoing service as a manager is tightly connected to the continued growth and engagement of your people. We're here to support you in rethinking traditional practices, attitudes, and habits, and adopting ones better suited to new ways of working and the digital workplace.

Splitting the role of the manager
Telstra, a $16 billion Australian telecommunications company that employs more than 32,000 people, has made perhaps the boldest move. When Telstra's CEO, Andy Penn, decided to make the company more customer-focused, fast-paced, and agile, he and his chief

human resources officer, Alex Badenoch, dramatically flattened its hierarchy, reducing the number of organizational layers to three.

Penn, Badenoch, and their team recognized that the restructuring provided a perfect opportunity to redesign the managerial job. "This change has been needed for so long," Badenoch told us. "We realized we had to separate work and management and create two distinct roles: *leader of people* and *leader of work.*" With very few exceptions, this new model applies to the entire organization.

Leaders of people are responsible for similarly skilled employees grouped into guildlike "chapters"—one for financial planners, say, and another for people experienced in change implementation. Most chapters consist of several hundred people, but some are larger. Subchapter leaders one level below are responsible for 15 to 20 members with narrower specializations and are located all over the world. What people do—not where they are—is what matters most.

Leaders of people ensure that the employees in their chapters have the skills and capabilities to meet the current and future needs of the business. They also help chapter members develop pathways to other chapters, to broaden insights and avoid silos. "The role of leaders of people," Badenoch told us, "is to know people beyond their work, to understand their career aspirations, to feed their minds and create thought provocations." Their performance is judged by such standards as how engaged they are with the people on their teams (measured by Net Promoter Scores) and how well they fulfill requirements, among them the amount of time that their people are actively at work on projects, as opposed to "on the bench."

Leaders of work focus on the flow of work and the commercial imperatives of the business. They don't directly manage people or control operating budgets. Instead, they create and execute work plans and determine which chapters to draw from for them. These leaders' performance is judged by such standards as the clarity of their planning, the quality of their estimates, and whether their projects are on time and on budget. (See the sidebar "Telstra's Dual Manager Model.")

Telstra's Dual Manager Model

TO BETTER COPE with what it calls the new "equation of work," the telecommunications firm Telstra has flattened its hierarchy and split the traditional role of manager into two jobs: one devoted to people and the other to process. The two types of managers are equals and coordinate closely with each other.

Leader of people	Leader of work
Leads a global chapter of employees with similar skills	Leads an agile project team drawn from chapters and external contractors
Owns the talent capacity, including personnel budgets	Owns the work, including project plans and budgets
Forecasts skills gaps and closes them through training and hiring	Forecasts demand for skills
Selects employees for projects	Bids for employees
Is responsible for employee engagement, career movement, and skills	Is responsible for project deliverables and business outcomes

This bold experiment has been widely acclaimed internally. "You actually get two people out of it who are dedicated to your development," one employee commented. "Your chapter lead [leader of people] is there to talk to you about your growth, and you get to have some great, powerful conversations about the type of work you want to do and how to get there. You can be very honest and share your aspirations openly with them. They have an amazing network and can get you assignments that allow you to explore different roles. And your project leader [leader of work] is there on a day-to-day basis to provide you direction on the work you need to do and on the business outcomes that we're trying to deliver."

At Telstra neither group of leaders is subordinate to the other. Their pay ranges are the same, and they participate as equals in the senior leadership team. Together they determine what Badenoch calls "the equation of work," which reveals "who is performing well, and what the skill and capacity is." Leaders of people have a sense of the dynamics of their talent pool, and leaders of work have a sense of the dynamics of workflow. By coordinating with their counterparts, leaders of people can anticipate skills gaps and prioritize training investments, or forecast undercapacity and the need for hiring—all while being mindful of the commitments, health, and well-being of employees.

This bifurcated model of management isn't new. It's been used for years in consulting, where one often finds a division between practice leadership and project leadership. What is new here is the context. Telstra has proven that the model can work effectively and profitably across all functions in big companies that have adopted agile practices and flexible work arrangements.

Let's step back and consider where we are. For roughly a century our approach to management was conventionally hierarchical. That made sense because work was organized sequentially and in silos, jobs were fixed, workspaces were physical, and information flowed downward. But that's no longer the case. In today's world of work, enabled by digitization, we prioritize agility, innovation, responsiveness, speed, and the value of human connection. All of that demands the new approach to management that we've discussed: one that involves shifts in power, skills, and structure.

We have to get this right. At no time in the past has the investor community paid such close attention to human capital in corporations—checking Glassdoor for signals of toxic work environments, demanding disclosure of metrics such as diversity and employee turnover. As the stewards of culture, managers are the lifeblood of organizations. The current state of overwhelmed, confused, and underskilled managers creates significant risk, not just to productivity and employee well-being but also to brand reputation.

Sometimes it takes a jolt like the new titles at Telstra and Standard Chartered, or the Manager Success Index at IBM, to signal that change is afoot. But in all cases the march to sustainable behavioral change is long. The Telstra experience shows us the benefits of a radical new organizational design, and the Standard Chartered and IBM experiences show us that at a minimum companies can take deliberate steps to shift managers' mindsets, energy, and focus. With these kinds of actions—which institutionalize change—we can ensure that people get the leadership they need in the new world of work.

Originally published in March–April 2022. Reprint R2202F

The Real Value of Middle Managers

by Zahira Jaser

THE IDEA OF MIDDLE MANAGERS as unexceptional, mediocre supervisors has been around for decades—at least since Abraham Zaleznik's seminal 1977 HBR article, "Managers and Leaders: Are They Different?," made a clear, explicit distinction between being a leader (an inspirational visionary) and being a manager (a strategic administrator). These ideas are still central to the concept taught in many MBA and executive development programs, where there's a tendency to educate managers on how to "upgrade" and become leaders.

In my 20 years of being a middle manager and then researching them, however, I have developed great respect for them. They are the engines of the business, the cogs that make things work, the glue that keeps companies together. As remote and hybrid work becomes more common—and the physical distance between employees increases—middle managers are more important than ever. The most effective ones possess humane, sophisticated communication skills and the knack to mediate and find common ground between actors at different organizational levels.

In fact, I believe that the so-called division between leadership and management is increasingly anachronistic, even becoming obsolete. It is time to reunite leadership and management in one concept and acknowledge middle managers as "connecting leaders," recognizing that every leader is also a follower and every follower is also a leader. Thus, a manager in the middle of hierarchical layers builds relationships with the people at the top (from a position of followership and lower power) and with those at the bottom (from a position of leadership and higher power).

This type of role is challenging, however, because it requires being both a proactive leader to direct reports and an engaged follower to the top management, all at the same time. Current ideas of leadership and training fail to capture this complex double act. For example, executive development programs focus on teaching leadership skills so managers can influence direct reports, largely ignoring the development of their upward influence skills. But it is directly through these double upward and downward influence activities that connecting leaders can shrink hierarchical distance and bring multiple levels of an organization together.

Based on years of research, I have identified four sets of practices that are key to creating successful connecting leaders. They are illustrated by the following four mini case studies, which outline

Four types of connecting leaders and practices

Connecting leader type	Practice	Main risk	Mitigator
Janus	Empathizing with both sides	Burnout and emotional labor	Coaching and psychological support
Broker	Negotiating with both sides to bring them together	Senior colleagues' lack of availability	Embracing a culture of transparency and humility
Conduit	Speaking up for others	Making oneself personally vulnerable to top management	Fostering a culture of psychological safety
Tightrope walker	Critically thinking about and appraising both sides of a dilemma	Cognitive overload, confusion, and being slow to take action	Encouraging safe critical-thinking spaces for peer discussions

Idea in Brief

Middle managers have long had a reputation as ineffective or weak supervisors. But research shows that, in fact, they're often the people who make an organization run smoothly across hierarchical levels. Especially today, as companies become more reliant on virtual modes of management and communication, investing in these managers as "connecting leaders" is vital. To do so, focus on four key types of connecting leaders and their associated practices. There are rewards and challenges for each, but successfully addressing them can help make your business more successful coming out of the pandemic.

both important practices and potential risks that companies and connecting leaders should be aware of when training in these roles. The case studies represent real managers I have interviewed, although their names have been changed for confidentiality.

The Connecting Leader as Janus

Janus is the Roman god depicted with two opposing faces. Essentially, a Janus leader engages with the concerns of partners at both higher and lower levels in an organization. This ability to look simultaneously up and down the hierarchy, in two directions, allows connecting leaders to empathize with the burdens of both sides and spread the weight of shared issues.

Chris is a seasoned middle manager in a large bank headquartered in London. He does not exude the charisma of a "heroic" leader: He is quietly self-confident, soft-spoken, and approachable. At the start of the pandemic, when emergency lockdown measures were deployed, he succeeded by maintaining this active double gaze, beginning with his employees:

> Now more than ever I need to make sure that everyone's voice is heard; the remoteness makes it easy for people to hide and shy away. But then again, everyone has got different circumstances, so you have to be more flexible around this. . . . You need to check in more regularly, and to reassure them.

And he kept his gaze trained upward toward his boss, ensuring that she was in the loop. By increasing the sharing of information, he shortened the hierarchical distance between himself, his boss, and his team:

> I have increased the frequency with which I hold regular catch-ups with the top. I have asked my boss to join calls with my direct reports sometimes so that she can answer questions from them. We can both be on the same page, have the same temperature check, get the raw message. This helps us respond quickly to concerns from the bottom.

Through his double gaze, Chris showed that to be a successful manager, it is not enough to simply be an effective leader—cherishing relationships with one's own reports from a position of higher authority—but it is also essential to be an engaged follower, involving and influencing one's own boss from a position of lower authority.

The greatest risks for Janus leaders like Chris are burnout and emotional labor. Because Chris is constantly empathizing with many different people at different organizational levels, it is important that he guard his energy and share the burdens with both sides. Organizations can mitigate this risk by offering coaching and psychological support so that managers can identify, discuss, and overcome this cognitive and emotional burden.

The Connecting Leader as a Broker

A broker creates a dialogue between people who have conflicting agendas. Because members of different hierarchical levels often have varying goals and needs, connecting leaders can serve as interpreters and translators of those needs, brokering cross-level dialogue between the people above and below them.

Sumiya, a middle manager in a private bank, couldn't give Mark, her star employee, the top ratings she thought he deserved in his latest performance review. Mark had been promoted the previous year, and Sumiya's boss, Paul, had indicated that top rankings were reserved for those destined for that year's promotion pool. She empathized with Mark's disappointment, recognizing the negative impact it could have on his motivation; she communicated this by avoiding being defensive when he brought it up with her. She knew she did not have full control in the decision process but realized that her ability to broker a meeting with Paul, a top executive, created an opportunity.

She set up a brief meeting between Mark and Paul. Mark had the chance to voice his disappointment and to hear Paul's rationale. The conversation with Paul boosted Mark's motivation:

> I went to speak to Paul about my disappointment, and he said, "I completely agree with why you're dissatisfied. You should deserve a four, but I had to give you a three." He was really open and honest about it and then continued, "We value you; this is a companywide decision, so don't be hard done by about that."

Sumiya's ability to broker the meeting, which cost Paul only 10 minutes, turned what could have been a negative event into a unifying one. Furthermore, Sumiya afforded Mark the opportunity to launch a fruitful relationship with Paul, stoking Mark's motivation and loyalty to the company.

The greatest risk for Sumiya, or any broker, is dealing with an uncooperative or unavailable executive, or one who is a challenge to win over. It's also possible for misunderstandings to occur during the attempt to bridge different parts of the organizational hierarchy. To mitigate this possibility, an organization can foster a culture of transparency and humility, in which top leadership accepts an open-door engagement with members in lower levels of the organization and embraces problems with a sense of compassion.

The Connecting Leader as a Conduit

Conduits courageously amplify the voices of their direct reports upward. These are often constructive challenges to those in positions of power, which can either trickle upward in a mediated way or be directly communicated from the bottom to the top.

To understand how this might play out, consider Simon, a risk management officer in a large financial firm, reporting to Mike, the head of risk at group level. Mike is sponsoring a revolutionary change program aimed at streamlining risk reporting across divisions. Simon uses his own voice to improve the implementation:

> I just have to remind Mike what it's like on the ground. Because he and his team on the 47th floor, they don't always have the opportunity to engage with people on the trading desks. Part of my team sits on the trading floor and they see the people, the business managers, and discuss things.

Furthermore, Simon facilitates the flow of his own direct reports' voices upward by allowing them to bring their input directly to Mike and his team:

> I get them directly involved in contributing their views because, at the end of the day, they will be buying in to the change. Yesterday I went upstairs with two of them and they explained (to Mike) why they were not happy, particularly on two things.

This took courage for Simon in two ways. First, by calling on his team members to help him persuade his boss, he was admitting that he was not always "the smartest guy in the room." Second, he amplified challenging points that might be at odds with his boss's agenda. In other words, he made himself vulnerable so that others could be heard. Research has shown that in order for employees to feel secure in speaking up, organizations need to foster a culture of psychological safety. This is vital for connecting leaders, who often have to voice concerns on behalf of others or encourage their employees to speak out for themselves.

The Connecting Leader as a Tightrope Walker

Finally, this type of connecting leader practice requires critically appraising and balancing dilemmas. The different, even opposing, needs and demands from colleagues at upper and lower levels present the connecting leader with myriad daily predicaments. For example, consider a manager who must design redundancy schemes while simultaneously keeping the team motivated, or who has to apply mechanisms of performance control while ensuring that team members have enough autonomy and drive in their positions to stay engaged. In these situations, connecting leaders run the risk of cognitive overload and paralysis. Critically and strategically thinking through the different sides of impasses and balancing them carefully will help connecting leaders avoid becoming overwhelmed.

Andrea is the head of a client-facing team in the sales division of a digital-marketing startup. As the founders scaled up and prepared to sell the startup, the company introduced a digital app, requiring salespeople to log every single client conversation. The sales team felt micromanaged from the top, and a rebellion ensued. Andrea found herself in a dilemma. On one hand, she thought the new system was counterproductive and limited the autonomy her people needed to achieve high performance:

> I don't want my people logging every conversation record on a computer. It serves no purpose, other than telling the founders that we've spoken to the client. My people are professionals; they know what they are doing.

On the other, she understood top management's need to push hard, as the company's valuation was directly tied to deals in the pipeline.

Andrea was extremely clear in presenting the dilemma and balancing the actions she decided to implement with her team:

> The trade-off is: OK, let's do it. It's a useful record, but minimize what you write! Let's be strategic about this.

Andrea's thought process and solution illustrate the skills that connecting leaders need for a constant balancing act, as they walk a tightrope between hierarchical layers. Risks to this practice include cognitive overload, confusion, and slow action, which can be mitigated by offering safe critical-thinking spaces for middle managers to debate among themselves, discussing pushback on top policies with peers. This is especially important when the company asks the most of them, such as implementing larger-scale strategic changes that require layoffs or restructuring.

How Companies Can Cultivate Connecting Leaders

In addition to the mitigation strategies already mentioned, organizations and executives can take three further measures to cultivate connecting leaders. Without them, connecting leaders may feel that doing and saying what's necessary is just too perilous.

Get company buy-in to support risk-taking

In order to recognize the sophisticated efforts of middle managers, highlight the four practices—empathizing, negotiating, speaking up, and balancing—as key performance indicators. This can be achieved through both executive buy-in and a companywide understanding of these practices.

Executive buy-in is important because much of what connecting leaders do is risky. It would be naive and idealistic to expect people to ramp up their performance in these areas without providing support. Remember: Some of these behaviors are riskier than others. For example, speaking up for others requires making yourself vulnerable to the top of the organization as well as possibly disappointing the bottom. So executives should prepare to aid connecting leaders by fostering an environment of psychological safety.

Once there is buy-in from the top, both the communications and human resources departments need to work together to update companywide language—for example, on balanced scorecards, hiring competencies lists, and contracts—to reflect the importance of these connecting behaviors. The balanced scorecards for executive performance should also be adjusted to reflect the importance of psychological safety and executives' coresponsibility of ensuring that connections are truly enabled.

Create development programs centered on both leadership and followership

First, development programs should be dedicated to unpacking, explaining, and teaching the abilities associated with each of the four practices. These programs should teach not only leadership skills (that is, how to influence those lower in the hierarchy) but also followership skills (how to influence those higher in the hierarchy).

In particular, the word "followership" sometimes connotes passivity. Development programs can aim squarely at making followership an active skill. One way is to design workshops that include managers from different levels reimagining and defining what it means to be active followers, sharing and reflecting on the difficulties of speaking up, influencing from below, and linking hierarchical levels. When I have run these types of sessions in an organization, I have witnessed transformation in the room and a sense of pride in being skilled at upward influencing. For connecting leaders, learning about and normalizing active, thoughtful followership is as important as learning about leadership.

Invest in better emotional support

Connecting leaders, given their strategic position, are often pulled in two directions—with emotional and cognitive costs. Especially during times of change, it is important to offer this population extra support, such as coaching and spaces for safe conversations and sharing. This measure is crucial for connecting leaders' success, but it is often undervalued by companies that spend more of the coaching budget on top executives than on middle managers.

———————

As hierarchies within companies become more fluid and virtual, middle managers will increasingly become channels for relationships, influence, and connection. For companies to be successful emerging from the pandemic, they need to recognize the complex and multifaceted role of middle managers, who are not just visionary, inspirational leaders but also courageous, engaged followers. Their ability to perform *both* upward and downward roles effectively requires them to develop sophisticated, humane skills to unite the layers of an organization.

Originally published on hbr.org on June 7, 2021. Reprint H06DWS

In Praise of Middle Managers

by Quy Nguyen Huy

THE VERY PHRASE "MIDDLE MANAGER" evokes mediocrity: a person who stubbornly defends the status quo because he's too unimaginative to dream up anything better—or, worse, someone who sabotages others' attempts to change the organization for the better.

The popular press and a couple generations' worth of change-management consultants have reinforced this stereotype. Introducing a major change initiative? Watch out for the middle managers—that's where you'll find the most resistance. Reengineering your business processes? Start by sweeping out the middle managers—they're just intermediaries; they don't add value. Until very recently, anyone who spent time reading about management practices, as opposed to watching real managers at work, might have concluded that middle managers are doomed to extinction or should be.

But don't pull out the pink slips just yet. I recently completed a six-year study of middle managers—in particular, their role during periods of radical organizational change. For the purposes of the study, I defined middle managers as any managers two levels below the CEO and one level above line workers and professionals. The research involved extensive on-site observations, in-depth interviews with more than 200 middle and senior managers, and a review of case research. My findings may surprise you.

Middle managers, it turns out, make valuable contributions to the realization of radical change at a company—contributions that go largely unrecognized by most senior executives. These contributions occur in four major areas. First, middle managers often have value-adding entrepreneurial ideas that they are able and willing to realize—if only they can get a hearing. Second, they're far better than most senior executives are at leveraging the informal networks at a company that make substantive, lasting change possible. Third, they stay attuned to employees' moods and emotional needs, thereby ensuring that the change initiative's momentum is maintained. And finally, they manage the tension between continuity and change—they keep the organization from falling into extreme inertia, on the one hand, or extreme chaos, on the other.

Of course, not every middle manager in every organization is a paragon of entrepreneurial vigor and energy. But I would argue that if senior managers dismiss the role that middle managers play—and carelessly reduce their ranks—they will drastically diminish their chances of realizing radical change. Indeed, middle managers may be corner-office executives' most effective allies when it's time to make a major change in a business. Let's take a closer look at their underestimated strengths.

The Entrepreneur

When it comes to envisioning and implementing change, middle managers stand in a unique organizational position. They're close to day-to-day operations, customers, and frontline employees—closer than senior managers are—so they know better than anyone where the problems are. But they're also far enough away from frontline work that they can see the big picture, which allows them to see new possibilities, both for solving problems and for encouraging growth. Taken as a group, middle managers are more diverse than their senior counterparts are in, for instance, functional area, work experience, geography, gender, and ethnic background. As a result, their insights are more diverse. Middle management is thus fertile ground for creative ideas about how to

Idea in Brief

The Myth

Middle managers have often been cast as dinosaurs, has-beens, and intermediaries who defend the status quo and resist attempts to change organizations for the better.

The Reality

Research shows that middle managers make valuable contributions to radical organizational change—and these contributions go largely unrecognized by senior executives. These contributions occur in four major areas:

- They often have good entrepreneurial ideas that they are able and willing to realize.

- They're better than most senior executives at leveraging the informal networks at companies that make substantive, lasting change.

- They stay attuned to employees' emotional needs during organizational change, sustaining momentum.

- They manage the tension between continuity and change, keeping the organization from falling into inertia or chaos.

While not every middle manager is a paragon of entrepreneurial vigor and energy, they may be executives' most effective allies when it's time to make major changes in businesses.

---

grow and change a business. In fact, middle managers' ideas are often better than their bosses' ideas.

Consider a large telecommunications company that I studied. When it initiated a radical change program a few years ago, 117 separate projects were funded. Of the projects that senior executives had proposed, 80% fell short of expectations or failed outright. Meanwhile, 80% of the projects that middle managers had initiated succeeded, bringing in at least $300 million in annual profits. In one of those projects, a 20-year veteran convinced senior managers that it made financial and operational sense to offer customers preventive maintenance on the network connections and infrastructures that the company sold and serviced. The concept was simple, but overcoming the political barriers to implement it was not. The middle manager, however, built support for the project one constituency at

Identifying Effective Middle Managers

MIDDLE MANAGERS ARE at least as important as senior executives in facilitating radical change, particularly if the company has suffered a major loss of institutional memory at the top. But it isn't always easy to identify the middle managers who will be most helpful.

My advice is to search for a small number of change agents deep in the organization. It is unrealistic to expect everybody to be instantly enthusiastic about a proposed change. The best one can hope for is early adoption and support from a critical few who can gradually spread the new ideas. These people aren't necessarily at the higher levels of the organization. Many senior executives confine themselves to looking only one level down from the top and conclude incorrectly that there are not enough people willing to change. They hire newcomers or consultants too quickly and put them in influential positions, exacerbating employees' feelings of misunderstanding and mistrust. As executives dig deeper in the organization, they should watch for the following qualities.

Look for Early Volunteers

Senior executives should enlist help from people at all levels who voluntarily come forward to participate in change initiatives. These individuals may have felt constrained under the previous regime and now see an opportunity to realize the changes they had promoted without success in the past. Such people are more numerous than one might think. The larger the organization, the more likely there are untapped talents with fresh ideas and a clear understanding of how things really get done.

Look for Positive Critics

Senior executives need people who are constructively critical, as opposed to inveterate naysayers and those who are wedded to the status quo. The difference is simple. Naysayers consistently find reasons why a change proposal won't work, and they are seldom, if ever, able to suggest a counterproposal and support it with evidence. By contrast, positive critics say: "I don't like your change proposal, and here's why. Let me suggest something else that could achieve the same results with less pain."

Look for People with Informal Power

These individuals' influence largely exceeds their formal authority; they're middle managers whose advice and help are highly sought after by people all around them. They have accumulated a lot of social capital inside the organization, are at the center of a large informal network, and know how to pull the right strings. They can become excellent ambassadors for change if senior executives can get them on board.

Look for Individuals Who Are Versatile

Versatile people have voluntarily adapted to relatively major changes in the past—things like shifts in career or geographic location. They are more likely to become early adopters if they think the change is aligned with their personal goals. If senior executives have trouble convincing this group, they are likely to experience much more difficulty with others.

Look for Emotional Intelligence

Individuals who are aware of their own emotions and those of others, and actively take steps to manage their feelings, are more likely to adapt to fresh environments. Research on emotional intelligence suggests that beyond a functional IQ threshold of 110 to 120, emotional intelligence is a much better predictor of social influence and success than IQ is—particularly in areas that demand high interpersonal skills. Managers with emotional self-awareness can take concrete actions that allow the whole organization to achieve high levels of adaptation and learning during radical change.[a]

Once you've identified potential allies in the middle-management ranks, put them to good use. Hold regular breakfast meetings and run your strategic thinking by them. Or develop a more formal advisory group. Pay attention to middle managers' interests and recognize their psychological needs. When people think that their intellectual and emotional worth is valued, they're far more likely to stay and help. In my research, I found many middle managers who dearly wanted to become "intrapreneurs"—to build something that could improve the organization's effectiveness and leave a lasting monument. Senior executives can help make that happen.

a. For more information, see my article, "Emotional Capability, Emotional Intelligence, and Radical Change," *Academy of Management Review,* April 1999; and my chapter "Emotional Capability and Corporate Change" in *Mastering Strategy: The Complete MBA Companion in Strategy* (Prentice Hall, 2000).

a time—first by appealing to his manager for the resources to prove that the idea was technically feasible, then by forming a small team to create prototype work processes and technologies, and finally by lobbying other groups in the organization to accept the change initiative. Ultimately, this project alone netted the company an estimated $10 million in profits during its first years.

Middle managers were equally successful at spurring innovation at other companies I studied. It was, for example, a middle-management team that developed Super Dry Beer, an innovative product that allowed Japanese brewer Asahi to capture new market share. That success set the stage for the struggling company's turnaround. And when Motorola needed to develop a wireless digital system for a client's cellular customers in less than a year—rather than the two or three years such projects typically took—it was, again, a team of middle managers that declared it could be done and did it.

At this point, you may be shaking your head, saying, "I'm not getting those kinds of results from my middle managers." And you may be right. But the problem most likely does not lie with your middle managers; it probably rests with you. Indeed, the more closely I looked at companies, the more examples I saw of senior executives failing to listen to their middle managers. Good ideas routinely died before they ever saw the light of day.

Why? An in-depth examination of several companies suggests that a vicious cycle is occurring. Today's businesspeople associate job mobility with adaptability; they value flexibility. Thus, veteran middle managers are considered corporate dinosaurs who will always offer a reason why something can't be achieved. For their part, senior managers believe this conventional wisdom and are reluctant to involve middle managers as trusted, knowledgeable advisers. Since they "know" middle managers are inherently resistant to change, they only pretend to listen to them. (Even the senior leaders who claim that middle managers should be included in strategic thinking rarely translate that rhetoric into action.) Middle managers, in turn, learn that they won't be listened to, so they take on the role of compliant child. They hide all their efforts to create change, knowing they will be penalized if they fail, and they don't push senior managers to pay attention. Matters are often complicated when external consultants are brought into the picture. They may suggest an approach that middle management has already tried—one that didn't work the first time, so it is likely to fail again. Furthermore, middle managers are predictably not enthusiastic about sharing their deep knowledge with consultants who display a better-than-thou attitude and cast the managers as fumbling has-beens to senior executives—mostly so the consultants can justify their own high fees and contract extensions. Middle managers too often have seen their good ideas fed to senior management by these same consultants, perhaps with more polish and better packaging than the middle managers would have used. Even if those ideas are pursued and successfully implemented, the middle managers don't get any credit, so the cycle continues.

Not getting credit is a pervasive problem. When the telecom company I studied embraced its radical change program, it had a new leadership team. The top managers very sensibly pushed the task of generating new ideas down to a group of long-standing middle managers, whose ideas turned out to be more grounded and profitable than the senior managers' ideas. But that's not how the outside world saw it. Shareholders and the media perceived that the new team had come in, cleaned up, and turned the company around. In a sense they had, but they hadn't done it alone, and they hadn't done it by cleaning house.

The Communicator

Aside from being an important source of entrepreneurial ideas, middle managers are also uniquely suited to communicating proposed changes across an organization. Change initiatives have two stages, conception and implementation, and it's widely understood that failure most often occurs at the second stage. What's less understood is the central role that middle managers play during this stage. Successful implementation requires clear and compelling communication throughout the organization. Middle managers can spread the word and get people on board because they usually have the best

Commitment—That Mysteriously Persistent Quality

MANY MIDDLE MANAGERS I studied could have found other jobs, often at higher pay. But something kept them from leaving—even though their workloads and their stress loads had often doubled as a result of the radical change being embraced. What kept them from leaving? In some cases, it was a sense of loyalty—they didn't want to desert their groups during a rough period. In other cases, their work and personal networks had become so intertwined that leaving would have created too large a loss. In still other cases, the sense of pulling together in a crisis created intense bonds similar to those that soldiers feel for one another. In all of those instances, though, I sensed an overarching commitment to the organization itself, or to middle managers' idea of the organization. The intensity with which managers wanted to protect the long-term interests of the company and the welfare of their subordinates surprised me again and again.

Many of them stayed, and most of them felt a deep connection to the company, but that doesn't mean they weren't conflicted. Quite the reverse: Many loyal company veterans felt hurt (in many cases, the company had unilaterally canceled their opportunities for lifetime employment) and guilt (they wanted to leave but couldn't imagine quitting midcourse and abandoning their subordinates). Often they distrusted new executives, disliked their transactional approaches to relationships, and disapproved of their short-term financial perspectives. Nonetheless, they stayed on board, worked 80 to 100 hours a week, and kept the company going. I don't altogether understand this loyalty—in many cases, it seemed undeserved and underappreciated—but I think it's important.

social networks in the company. Many of them start their careers as operations workers or technical specialists. Over time and through various job rotations at the same company, they build webs of relationships that are both broad and deep. They know who really knows what and how to get things done. Typically their networks include unwritten obligations and favors traded, giving effective middle managers a significant amount of informal leverage.

Senior managers have their own networks, of course, but these tend to be less powerful because many of these executives have been at their companies for shorter periods of time. For instance, at the telecom company I cited earlier, most of the executives had less than four years' tenure. By contrast, most of the middle managers had been with the company for more than eight years—and it was not uncommon to see a middle manager with up to 30 years' tenure. Other companies in my research sample displayed a similar pattern.

Don't underestimate these tenure figures. Employees often grouse about radical change initiatives because they perceive that the "new guy" doesn't understand operations well enough to upend their routines. When that happens, the incoming executive's fresh ideas don't have a prayer of succeeding unless they're married to the operating skills—and credibility—of veteran middle managers.

For example, when new executives were charged with turning around Hewlett-Packard's Santa Rosa Systems division, which produces test and measurement equipment for electronic systems, they enlisted a task force of eight middle managers to collect employees' views about the current leadership (negative) and customers' views about the division's performance (also negative). The result was candid, detailed feedback that sometimes felt like "an icy bucket of water over the head," as one executive described it, but that also allowed executives to adjust their change proposals on the fly. Middle managers were consulted early and often about strategic and operational questions. As a result, they understood better what the senior team was trying to accomplish and felt more comfortable supporting executives' intentions. The end result was one of the speediest turnarounds ever of an HP division.

If the middle managers with the best networks—and the most credibility—genuinely buy into the change program, they'll sell it to the rest of the organization in subtle and non-threatening ways. And they'll know which groups or individuals most need to be on board and how to customize the message for different audiences. When one company needed to change the way that it delivered telecommunications services to customers, for example, a middle manager in engineering sought help from his colleagues in sales and operations. He'd known employees in both groups for years; he drew on those long-term relationships, and his colleagues were able to convince their constituencies to lend the engineering manager support for the change. Working through these intermediaries proved critical to the success and speed of implementation.

As they tap into their networks, middle managers use keen translation skills to sell a change initiative throughout a work group or a company. At a large public utility that I studied, which is undergoing deregulation, a middle manager had to explain the radical changes that top managers were proposing in language his people would understand. He quickly realized that official discourse held little sway with these people, who were inclined to be cynical about organizational change. So he actively engaged his workers, one by one, outside of the office, in a social or sports milieu where they were more relaxed. He customized the change message in a way that was personally meaningful to each individual. This unexpected gesture pleasantly surprised employees, who were used to more hierarchical, formal relationships, and it weakened their resistance to the changes being proposed.

Other middle managers use local intermediaries—ambassadors who are considered trustworthy by their peers and can sell the idea of radical change in a friendly way. So a disruptive change in work processes would be described to finance managers in terms of a discounted pay-back period on investment or a head-count reduction, and it would be explained to operations managers in terms of fewer complaints about service disruption. Same story, different emphasis.

Sometimes senior executives themselves can be barriers to change, and it requires tactful communication by middle managers to keep the company on track. For instance, a middle manager at a large airline I studied realized that most of the senior executives barely knew how to use a PC. Few of them understood the capabilities or limitations of the Web well enough to make complex strategic decisions about the company's use of the Internet and e-commerce. To educate them, the middle manager developed a reverse-mentoring program: Younger employees would teach experienced executives about the Internet. In turn, the executives would expose their young mentors to more senior-level business issues, decisions, and practices. Each member of the pair was separated by several hierarchical levels, and each came from different business units. The middle manager correctly assumed that this degree of separation would make the executives more comfortable about admitting their weaknesses with computers. The program was a success; eventually, hundreds of executives at the airline became more technology literate and less fearful of change.

As that example demonstrates, middle managers' understanding of outside market pressures and internal sensitivities and capabilities allows them to evaluate the relevance and feasibility of proposed corporate changes.

The Therapist

Radical changes in the workplace can stir up high levels of fear among employees. Uncertainty about change can deflate morale and trigger anxiety that, unchecked, can degenerate into depression and paralysis. Once people are depressed, they stop learning, adapting, or helping to move the group forward. Senior managers can't do much to alleviate this pain; they're too removed from most workers to help, and they're also focused externally more than internally.

Middle managers, though, have no choice but to address their employees' emotional well-being during times of radical change. If they ignore it, most useful work will come to a grinding halt as people either leave the company or become afraid to act. Even as they privately deplore the lack of attention from their own bosses, many middle managers make sure that their own sense of alienation doesn't seep down to their subordinates. They do a host of things to create a psychologically safe work environment. They're able to do this, once again, because of their position within the organization. They know the people who report to them—as well as those reports' direct reports—and they can communicate directly and personally, rather than in vague corporate-speak. They can also tailor individual conversations to individual needs. Some employees will have big concerns about whether a new strategic direction is right for the organization; others will be far more interested in whether they're going to be forced to move or to give up a flexible schedule.

One manager I interviewed recalled the kinds of support his direct reports required when they faced possible relocation to Texas. A service representative at the company announced in a public meeting that she couldn't move to Dallas immediately; in private, she explained that she was going through a divorce. Another service rep was concerned that she wouldn't be able to find a special-needs school for her child in the new location. Others had sick parents. "Relocation is a very emotional thing," the middle manager said. "So we . . . paid [for] visits to the new location a few months in advance. The [company's] welcoming party appointed sponsors to every family—to look after their personal needs, to take them out to dinner the first weeks, or to find a baseball team for the kids."

As his comments suggest, middle managers shoulder substantial additional burdens during a period of profound change. Besides the already challenging daily tasks of operations and revenue generation, they provide far more hand-holding, practical problem solving, and support than they usually do. (See the sidebar "Compassion Fatigue Is Real.")

In some cases, middle managers conclude that proposed changes are so profoundly disquieting that their groups will benefit from outside, professional help. I attended a full-day session, set up by middle managers, in which workers at a company that was facing rapid downsizing broke into small groups, drew pictures about how they were feeling collectively, looked at one another's pictures, and laughed about how awful things were. Toward the end of the day, the consultants walked them through Elisabeth Kubler-Ross's model of bereavement, which put their feelings into a coherent context. My initial skepticism about the use of such a touchy-feely approach faded when frontline workers told me, over the next few weeks, how much more energy they had for their work after they'd expressed their feelings. Employee surveys conducted several months later confirmed the improvement in employee morale.

As that experience indicates, employees often help one another through hard times. Indeed, the stress and anxiety aroused by radical change increases the likelihood of altruistic behavior among people who have been with an organization—and one another—for

Compassion Fatigue Is Real

by Dina Denham Smith

DO YOU EVER FIND THAT your empathy ebbs and flows? During some moments you're able to support your team through emotionally trying times, but during others you're just going through the motions, secretly numb to the obstacles they face.

If this is true for you, don't feel ashamed. Your feelings (or lack thereof) are valid. Helping others who are in pain is a prosocial response, but it can be taxing and over time it can result in *compassion fatigue.*[a]

Sometimes mistaken for burnout, compassion fatigue is the physical, emotional, and psychological impact of helping others. Often experienced by professionals tasked with supporting people through stress and trauma, such as doctors or therapists, the condition is marked by exhaustion, negative emotions, and loss of empathy. In the medical field, according to psychologist Heidi Allespach, "caregivers can become so over-empathic that they find themselves growing numb to their patients' suffering."[b]

Since the pandemic, we have been seeing more of this in the workplace as well. Leaders and managers have been asked to double down on empathy in support of team members recovering from grief, loss, and lapses in mental health. They have been asked to be more sensitive—to shoulder new emotional burdens while navigating exceptional levels of uncertainty and doing more with less. While this has been the order of the day and most managers have answered the call, it has come at a cost.

The pandemic has receded for the most part, but the emotional demand on leaders is still large. Employees expect compassionate managers and sustainable, mentally healthy workplaces—and are ready to quit when these expectations aren't fulfilled.

Whether you are a first-time manager or a seasoned leader, in order to meet these standards and safeguard your own well-being you need to prioritize your own mental health and wellness. That way you can face the emotional demands of leading your team through the stress of today's world.

a. C.R. Figley, "Compassion Fatigue: Toward a New Understanding of the Costs of Caring," in B.H. Stamm (ed.), *Secondary Traumatic Stress: Self-Care Issues for Clinicians, Researchers, and Educators* (Lutherville, MD: The Sidran Press, 1999): 3–28.

b. Rebecca A. Clay, "Are You Experiencing Compassion Fatigue?" American Psychological Association, July 11, 2022, https://www.apa.org/topics/covid-19/compassion-fatigue.

Adapted from "Compassion Fatigue Is Real and It May Be Weighing You Down," on hbr.org, March 30, 2022.

a long time. Being able to help a colleague can reduce any feelings of pain and dread in the helper. A good middle manager will encourage this behavior, keep it positive, and use it to keep work on track.

The Tightrope Artist

Successful organizational change requires attention not only to employee morale but also to the balance between change and continuity. If too much change happens too fast, chaos ensues. If too little change happens too slowly, it results in organizational inertia. Both extremes can lead to severe underperformance. Even during normal times, middle managers allot considerable energy to finding the right mix of the two. When radical change is being imposed from the top, this balancing act becomes even more important—and far more difficult.

Middle managers, like the people who report to them, are overburdened and stressed out during periods of profound change—but I noticed that they found personal and professional fulfillment by taking on this particular balancing act. They're problem solvers, typically, and they find relief in rolling up their sleeves and figuring out how to make the whole messy thing work. They don't all do it the same way, of course—and, from a senior-management point of view, that's a good thing. Some middle managers pay more attention to the continuity side of the equation, and some tend more to the change side.

We've already looked at what middle managers do to ensure continuity. They "keep the company working," as one of them said to me with some pride. At the telecom company I studied, middle managers' focus on continuity contributed to a relatively smooth downsizing of 13,000 positions. By showing flexibility and fairness, and by working closely with union representatives, managers defused resentment and avoided a strike. Their concern for employees kept anxiety at manageable levels. Their loyalty to the organization probably slowed turnover rates. And as a result of the middle managers' actions, the telecom company was able to generate revenues at decent levels during an extraordinarily difficult time, thus providing needed cash for the multitude of change projects. Other middle managers are more interested in promoting change. They champion projects, putting intense pressure on the people who control resources and equally intense pressure on their own people. At the telecom company, these change champions pushed their own people, and eventually the whole organization, into developing a new set of tools to change their work processes—for instance, new technologies for managing risk, ensuring quality, and segmenting customers. But that didn't go smoothly; employees balked at the change. The middle managers went through a learning process themselves. Because they wanted to make changes happen quickly, they imposed these new tools abruptly, with little psychological preparation. They had to start over. The second time around they involved more people at the middle and lower levels of the division, with more gradual discussion, small-scale trials, and continuous fine-tuning. This exercise of "learning how to change," as painful as it was, may have been the most important lesson for these middle managers. As some of them remarked, learning from failure can be the most memorable way to build skills.

Turnover among top executives is higher today than it's ever been, and that's unlikely to change anytime soon. But that isn't necessarily a bad thing. After all, the business landscape is changing very quickly, and the CEO who championed a major shift in strategic direction 10 years ago is probably not going to be able to do the same thing again.

But the new executive who wants to introduce radical change can't simply come in and clean house, because the job isn't actually to reinvent the company from the ground up.

The challenge is more complex than that: It's figuring out how to hold on to core values and capabilities while simultaneously changing how work gets done and shifting the organization in new strategic directions. This simply won't happen unless people throughout the organization help make it happen. Middle managers understand—in a deep way—those core values and competencies. They're the ones who can translate and synthesize; who can implement strategy because they know how to get things done; who can keep work groups from spinning into alienated, paralyzed chaos; and who can be persuaded to put their credibility on the line to turn vision into reality.

The senior executive who learns to recognize, respect, and deal fairly with the most influential middle managers in an organization will gain trusted allies—and improve the odds of realizing a complex but necessary organizational change.

Originally published in September 2001. Reprint R0108D

Managing Your Boss

by John J. Gabarro and John P. Kotter

TO MANY PEOPLE, THE PHRASE "managing your boss" may sound unusual or suspicious. Because of the traditional top-down emphasis in most organizations, it is not obvious why you need to manage relationships upward—unless, of course, you would do so for personal or political reasons. But we are not referring to political maneuvering or to apple polishing. We are using the term to mean the process of consciously working with your superior to obtain the best possible results for you, your boss, and the company.

Recent studies suggest that effective managers take time and effort to manage not only relationships with their subordinates but also those with their bosses. These studies also show that this essential aspect of management is sometimes ignored by otherwise talented and aggressive managers. Indeed, some managers who actively and effectively supervise subordinates, products, markets, and technologies assume an almost passively reactive stance vis-à-vis their bosses. Such a stance almost always hurts them and their companies.

If you doubt the importance of managing your relationship with your boss or how difficult it is to do so effectively, consider for a moment the following sad but telling story:

Frank Gibbons was an acknowledged manufacturing genius in his industry and, by any profitability standard, a very effective executive. In 1973, his strengths propelled him into the position of vice president of manufacturing for the second largest and most profitable company in its industry. Gibbons was not, however, a good manager of people. He knew this, as did others in his company and his industry. Recognizing this weakness, the president made sure that those who reported to Gibbons were good at working with people and could compensate for his limitations. The arrangement worked well.

In 1975, Philip Bonnevie was promoted into a position reporting to Gibbons. In keeping with the previous pattern, the president selected Bonnevie because he had an excellent track record and a reputation for being good with people. In making that selection, however, the president neglected to notice that, in his rapid rise through the organization, Bonnevie had always had good-to-excellent bosses. He had never been forced to manage a relationship with a difficult boss. In retrospect, Bonnevie admits he had never thought that managing his boss was a part of his job.

Fourteen months after he started working for Gibbons, Bonnevie was fired. During that same quarter, the company reported a net loss for the first time in seven years. Many of those who were close to these events say that they don't really understand what happened. This much is known, however: While the company was bringing out a major new product—a process that required sales, engineering, and manufacturing groups to coordinate decisions very carefully—a whole series of misunderstandings and bad feelings developed between Gibbons and Bonnevie.

For example, Bonnevie claims Gibbons was aware of and had accepted Bonnevie's decision to use a new type of machinery to make the new product; Gibbons swears he did not. Furthermore, Gibbons claims he made it clear to Bonnevie that the introduction of the product was too important to the company in the short run to take any major risks.

As a result of such misunderstandings, planning went awry: A new manufacturing plant was built that could not produce the new product designed by engineering, in the volume desired by sales, at a cost agreed on by the executive committee. Gibbons blamed Bonnevie for the mistake. Bonnevie blamed Gibbons.

Idea in Brief

Managing our *bosses*? Isn't that merely manipulation? Corporate cozying up? Out-and-out apple polishing? In fact, we manage our bosses for very good reasons: to get resources to do the best job, not only for ourselves, but for our bosses and our companies as well. We actively pursue a healthy and productive working relationship based on mutual respect and understanding—understanding our own and our bosses' strengths, weaknesses, goals, work styles, and needs. Here's what can happen when we don't:

Example: A new president with a formal work style replaced someone who'd been looser, more intuitive. The new president preferred written reports and structured meetings. One of his managers found this too controlling. He seldom sent background information, and was often blindsided by unanticipated questions. His boss found their meetings inefficient and frustrating. The manager had to resign.

In contrast, here's how another manager's sensitivity to this same boss's style really paid off:

Example: This manager identified the kinds and frequency of information the president wanted. He sent ahead background reports and discussion agendas. The result? Highly productive meetings and even more innovative problem solving than with his previous boss.

Managers often don't realize how much their bosses depend on them. They need cooperation, reliability, and honesty from their direct reports. Many managers also don't realize how much *they* depend on their bosses—for links to the rest of the organization, for setting priorities, and for obtaining critical resources.

Recognizing this mutual dependence, effective managers seek out information about the boss's concerns and are sensitive to his work style. They also understand how their own attitudes toward authority can sabotage the relationship. Some see the boss as the enemy and fight him at every turn; others are overly compliant, viewing the boss as an all-wise parent.

Of course, one could argue that the problem here was caused by Gibbons's inability to manage his subordinates. But one can make just as strong a case that the problem was related to Bonnevie's inability to manage his boss. Remember, Gibbons was not having difficulty with any other subordinates. Moreover, given the personal

Idea in Practice

You can benefit from this mutual dependence and develop a very productive relationship with your boss by focusing on:

- **Compatible work styles.** Bosses process information differently. "Listeners" prefer to be briefed in person so they can ask questions. "Readers" want to process written information first, and then meet to discuss.

Decision-making styles also vary. Some bosses are highly involved. Touch base with them frequently. Others prefer to delegate. Inform them about important decisions you've already made.

- **Mutual expectations.** Don't passively assume you know what the boss expects. Find out. With some bosses, write detailed outlines of your work for their approval. With others, carefully planned discussions are key.

Also, communicate *your* expectations to find out if they are realistic. Persuade the boss to accept the most important ones.

- **Information flow.** Managers typically underestimate what their bosses need to know—and what they *do* know. Keep the boss informed through processes that fit his style. Be forthright about both good and bad news.

- **Dependability and honesty.** Trustworthy subordinates only make promises they can keep and don't shade the truth or play down difficult issues.

- **Good use of time and resources.** Don't waste your boss's time with trivial issues. Selectively draw on his time and resources to meet the most important goals—yours, his, and the company's.

price paid by Bonnevie (being fired and having his reputation within the industry severely tarnished), there was little consolation in saying the problem was that Gibbons was poor at managing subordinates. Everyone already knew that.

We believe that the situation could have turned out differently had Bonnevie been more adept at understanding Gibbons and at managing his relationship with him. In this case, an inability to manage upward was unusually costly. The company lost $2 million to $5 million, and Bonnevie's career was, at least temporarily, disrupted. Many less costly cases similar to this probably occur regularly in all major corporations, and the cumulative effect can be very destructive.

Misreading the Boss–Subordinate Relationship

People often dismiss stories like the one we just related as being merely cases of personality conflict. Because two people can on occasion be psychologically or temperamentally incapable of working together, this can be an apt description. But more often, we have found, a personality conflict is only a part of the problem—sometimes a very small part.

Bonnevie did not just have a different personality from Gibbons, he also made or had unrealistic assumptions and expectations about the very nature of boss-subordinate relationships. Specifically, he did not recognize that his relationship to Gibbons involved *mutual dependence* between two *fallible* human beings. Failing to recognize this, a manager typically either avoids trying to manage his or her relationship with a boss or manages it ineffectively.

Some people behave as if their bosses were not very dependent on them. They fail to see how much the boss needs their help and cooperation to do his or her job effectively. These people refuse to acknowledge that the boss can be severely hurt by their actions and needs cooperation, dependability, and honesty from them.

Some people see themselves as not very dependent on their bosses. They gloss over how much help and information they need from the boss in order to perform their own jobs well. This superficial view is particularly damaging when a manager's job and decisions affect other parts of the organization, as was the case in Bonnevie's situation. A manager's immediate boss can play a critical role in linking the manager to the rest of the organization, making sure the manager's priorities are consistent with organizational needs, and in securing the resources the manager needs to perform well. Yet some managers need to see themselves as practically self-sufficient, as not needing the critical information and resources a boss can supply.

Many managers, like Bonnevie, assume that the boss will magically know what information or help their subordinates need and provide it to them. Certainly, some bosses do an excellent job of caring for their subordinates in this way, but for a manager to expect that from all bosses is dangerously unrealistic. A more reasonable expectation for managers to have is that modest help will be forthcoming. After all, bosses are only human. Most really effective managers accept this fact and assume primary responsibility for their own careers and development. They make a point of seeking the information and help they need to do a job instead of waiting for their bosses to provide it.

In light of the foregoing, it seems to us that managing a situation of mutual dependence among fallible human beings requires the following:

1. You have a good understanding of the other person and yourself, especially regarding strengths, weaknesses, work styles, and needs.

2. You use this information to develop and manage a healthy working relationship—one that is compatible with both people's work styles and assets, is characterized by mutual expectations, and meets the most critical needs of the other person.

This combination is essentially what we have found highly effective managers doing.

Understanding the Boss

Managing your boss requires that you gain an understanding of the boss and his or her context, as well as your own situation. All managers do this to some degree, but many are not thorough enough.

At a minimum, you need to appreciate your boss's goals and pressures, his or her strengths and weaknesses. What are your boss's organizational and personal objectives, and what are his or her pressures, especially those from his or her own boss and others at the same level? What are your boss's long suits and blind spots? What is the preferred style of working? Does your boss like to get information through memos, formal meetings, or phone calls? Does he or she thrive on conflict or try to minimize it? Without this information, a manager is flying blind when dealing with the boss, and unnecessary conflicts, misunderstandings, and problems are inevitable.

In one situation we studied, a top-notch marketing manager with a superior performance record was hired into a company as a vice president "to straighten out the marketing and sales problems." The company, which was having financial difficulties, had recently been acquired by a larger corporation. The president was eager to turn it around and gave the new marketing vice president free rein—at least initially. Based on his previous experience, the new vice president correctly diagnosed that greater market share was needed for the company and that strong product management was required to bring that about. Following that logic, he made a number of pricing decisions aimed at increasing high-volume business.

When margins declined and the financial situation did not improve, however, the president increased pressure on the new vice president. Believing that the situation would eventually correct itself as the company gained back market share, the vice president resisted the pressure.

When by the second quarter, margins and profits had still failed to improve, the president took direct control over all pricing decisions and put all items on a set level of margin, regardless of volume. The new vice president began to find himself shut out by the president, and their relationship deteriorated. In fact, the vice president found the president's behavior bizarre. Unfortunately, the president's new pricing scheme also failed to increase margins, and by the fourth quarter, both the president and the vice president were fired.

What the new vice president had not known until it was too late was that improving marketing and sales had been only *one* of the president's goals. His most immediate goal had been to make the company more profitable—quickly.

Nor had the new vice president known that his boss was invested in this short-term priority for personal as well as business reasons. The president had been a strong advocate of the acquisition within the parent company, and his personal credibility was at stake.

The vice president made three basic errors. He took information supplied to him at face value, he made assumptions in areas where he had no information, and—what was most damaging—he never actively tried to clarify what his boss's objectives were. As a result, he ended up taking actions that were actually at odds with the president's priorities and objectives.

Managers who work effectively with their bosses do not behave this way. They seek out information about the boss's goals and problems and pressures. They are alert for opportunities to question the boss and others around him or her to test their assumptions. They pay attention to clues in the boss's behavior. Although it is imperative that they do this especially when they begin working with a new boss, effective managers also do this on an ongoing basis because they recognize that priorities and concerns change.

Being sensitive to a boss's work style can be crucial, especially when the boss is new. For example, a new president who was organized and formal in his approach replaced a man who was informal and intuitive. The new president worked best when he had written reports. He also preferred formal meetings with set agendas.

One of his division managers realized this need and worked with the new president to identify the kinds and frequency of information and reports that the president wanted. This manager also made a point of sending background information and brief agendas ahead of time for their discussions. He found that with this type of preparation their meetings were very useful. Another interesting result was, he found that with adequate preparation his new boss was even more effective at brainstorming problems than his more informal and intuitive predecessor had been.

In contrast, another division manager never fully understood how the new boss's work style differed from that of his predecessor. To the degree that he did sense it, he experienced it as too much control. As a result, he seldom sent the new president the background information he needed, and the president never felt fully prepared for meetings with the manager. In fact, the president spent much of the time when they met trying to get information that he felt he should have had earlier. The boss experienced these meetings as frustrating and inefficient, and the subordinate often found himself thrown off guard by the questions that the president asked. Ultimately, this division manager resigned.

The difference between the two division managers just described was not so much one of ability or even adaptability. Rather, one of the men was more sensitive to his boss's work style and to the implications of his boss's needs than the other was.

Understanding Yourself

The boss is only one-half of the relationship. You are the other half, as well as the part over which you have more direct control. Developing an effective working relationship requires, then, that you know your own needs, strengths and weaknesses, and personal style.

You are not going to change either your basic personality structure or that of your boss. But you can become aware of what it is about you that impedes or facilitates working with your boss and, with that awareness, take actions that make the relationship more effective.

For example, in one case we observed, a manager and his superior ran into problems whenever they disagreed. The boss's typical response was to harden his position and overstate it. The manager's reaction was then to raise the ante and intensify the forcefulness of his argument. In doing this, he channeled his anger into sharpening his attacks on the logical fallacies he saw in his boss's assumptions. His boss in turn would become even more adamant about holding his original position. Predictably, this escalating cycle resulted in the subordinate avoiding whenever possible any topic of potential conflict with his boss.

In discussing this problem with his peers, the manager discovered that his reaction to the boss was typical of how he generally reacted to counterarguments—but with a difference. His response would overwhelm his peers but not his boss. Because his attempts to discuss this problem with his boss were unsuccessful, he concluded that the only way to change the situation was to deal with his own instinctive reactions. Whenever the two reached an impasse, he would check his own impatience and suggest that they break up and think about it before getting together again. Usually when they renewed their discussion, they had digested their differences and were more able to work them through.

Gaining this level of self-awareness and acting on it are difficult but not impossible. For example, by reflecting over his past experiences, a young manager learned that he was not very good at dealing with difficult and emotional issues where people were involved. Because he disliked those issues and realized that his instinctive responses to them were seldom very good, he developed a habit of touching base with his boss whenever such a problem arose. Their discussions always surfaced ideas and approaches the manager had not considered. In many cases, they also identified specific actions the boss could take to help.

Although a superior-subordinate relationship is one of mutual dependence, it is also one in which the subordinate is typically more dependent on the boss than the other way around. This dependence inevitably results in the subordinate feeling a certain degree of frustration, sometimes anger, when his actions or options are constrained by his boss's decisions. This is a normal part of life and occurs in the best of relationships. The way in which a manager handles these frustrations largely depends on his or her predisposition toward dependence on authority figures.

Some people's instinctive reaction under these circumstances is to resent the boss's authority and to rebel against the boss's decisions. Sometimes a person will escalate a conflict beyond what is appropriate. Seeing the boss almost as an institutional enemy, this type of manager will often, without being conscious of it, fight with the boss just for the sake of fighting. The subordinate's reactions to being constrained are usually strong and sometimes impulsive. He or she sees the boss as someone who, by virtue of the role, is a hindrance to progress, an obstacle to be circumvented or at best tolerated.

Psychologists call this pattern of reactions counterdependent behavior. Although a counterdependent person is difficult for most superiors to manage and usually has a history of strained relationships with superiors, this sort of manager is apt to have even more trouble with a boss who tends to be directive or authoritarian. When the manager acts on his or her negative feelings, often in subtle and nonverbal ways, the boss sometimes does become the enemy. Sensing the subordinate's latent hostility, the boss will lose trust in the subordinate or his or her judgment and then behave even less openly.

Paradoxically, a manager with this type of predisposition is often a good manager of his or her own people. He or she will many times go out of the way to get support for them and will not hesitate to go to bat for them.

At the other extreme are managers who swallow their anger and behave in a very compliant fashion when the boss makes what they know to be a poor decision. These managers will agree with the boss even when a disagreement might be welcome or when the boss would easily alter a decision if given more information. Because they bear no relationship to the specific situation at hand, their responses are as much an overreaction as those of counterdependent managers. Instead of seeing the boss as an enemy, these people deny their anger—the other extreme—and tend to see the boss as if he or she were an all-wise parent who should know best, should take responsibility for their careers, train them in all they need to know, and protect them from overly ambitious peers.

Both counterdependence and overdependence lead managers to hold unrealistic views of what a boss is. Both views ignore that bosses, like everyone else, are imperfect and fallible. They don't have unlimited time, encyclopedic knowledge, or extrasensory perception; nor are they evil enemies. They have their own pressures and concerns that are sometimes at odds with the wishes of the subordinate—and often for good reason.

Altering predispositions toward authority, especially at the extremes, is almost impossible without intensive psychotherapy (psychoanalytic theory and research suggest that such predispositions are deeply rooted in a person's personality and upbringing). However, an awareness of these extremes and the range between them can be very useful in understanding where your own predispositions fall and what the implications are for how you tend to behave in relation to your boss.

If you believe, on the one hand, that you have some tendencies toward counterdependence, you can understand and even predict what your reactions and overreactions are likely to be. If, on the other hand, you believe you have some tendencies toward overdependence, you might question the extent to which your overcompliance or inability to confront real differences may be making both you and your boss less effective.

Developing and Managing the Relationship

With a clear understanding of both your boss and yourself, you can *usually* establish a way of working together that fits both of you, that is characterized by unambiguous mutual expectations, and that helps you both be more productive and effective. The "Checklist for managing your boss" summarizes some things such a relationship consists of. Following are a few more.

Checklist for managing your boss

Make sure you understand your boss and his or her context, including:

☐ Goals and objectives

☐ Pressures

☐ Strengths, weaknesses, blind spots

☐ Preferred work style

Assess yourself and your needs, including:

☐ Strengths and weaknesses

☐ Personal style

☐ Predisposition toward dependence on authority figures

Develop and maintain a relationship that:

☐ Fits both your needs and styles

☐ Is characterized by mutual expectations

☐ Keeps your boss informed

☐ Is based on dependability and honesty

☐ Selectively uses your boss's time and resources

Compatible work styles

Above all else, a good working relationship with a boss accommo-
dates differences in work style. For example, in one situation we
studied, a manager (who had a relatively good relationship with his
superior) realized that during meetings his boss would often become
inattentive and sometimes brusque. The subordinate's own style
tended to be discursive and exploratory. He would often digress
from the topic at hand to deal with background factors, alternative
approaches, and so forth. His boss preferred to discuss problems
with a minimum of background detail and became impatient and
distracted whenever his subordinate digressed from the immediate
issue.

Recognizing this difference in style, the manager became terser
and more direct during meetings with his boss. To help himself do
this, before meetings, he would develop brief agendas that he used
as a guide. Whenever he felt that a digression was needed, he explained why. This small shift in his own style made these meetings
more effective and far less frustrating for both of them.

Subordinates can adjust their styles in response to their bosses'
preferred method for receiving information. Peter Drucker di-
vides bosses into "listeners" and "readers." Some bosses like to
get information in report form so they can read and study it. Others work better with information and reports presented in person
so they can ask questions. As Drucker points out, the implications
are obvious. If your boss is a listener, you brief him or her in person, *then* follow it up with a memo. If your boss is a reader, you
cover important items or proposals in a memo or report, *then* discuss
them.

Other adjustments can be made according to a boss's decision-
making style. Some bosses prefer to be involved in decisions
and problems as they arise. These are high-involvement managers
who like to keep their hands on the pulse of the operation. Usually their needs (and your own) are best satisfied if you touch base
with them on an ad hoc basis. A boss who has a need to be involved
will become involved one way or another, so there are advantages
to including him or her at your initiative. Other bosses prefer to

delegate—they don't want to be involved. They expect you to come to them with major problems and inform them about any important changes.

Creating a compatible relationship also involves drawing on each other's strengths and making up for each other's weaknesses. Because he knew that the boss—the vice president of engineering—was not very good at monitoring his employees' problems, one manager we studied made a point of doing it himself. The stakes were high: The engineers and technicians were all union members, the company worked on a customer-contract basis, and the company had recently experienced a serious strike.

The manager worked closely with his boss, along with people in the scheduling department and the personnel office, to make sure that potential problems were avoided. He also developed an informal arrangement through which his boss would review with him any proposed changes in personnel or assignment policies before taking action. The boss valued his advice and credited his subordinate for improving both the performance of the division and the labor-management climate.

Mutual expectations

The subordinate who passively assumes that he or she knows what the boss expects is in for trouble. Of course, some superiors will spell out their expectations very explicitly and in great detail. But most do not. And although many corporations have systems that provide a basis for communicating expectations (such as formal planning processes, career planning reviews, and performance appraisal reviews), these systems never work perfectly. Also, between these formal reviews, expectations invariably change.

Ultimately, the burden falls on the subordinate to find out what the boss's expectations are. They can be both broad (such as what kinds of problems the boss wishes to be informed about and when) as well as very specific (such things as when a particular project should be completed and what kinds of information the boss needs in the interim).

Getting a boss who tends to be vague or not explicit to express expectations can be difficult. But effective managers find ways to get that information. Some will draft a detailed memo covering key aspects of their work and then send it to their boss for approval. They then follow this up with a face-to-face discussion in which they go over each item in the memo. A discussion like this will often surface virtually all of the boss's expectations.

Other effective managers will deal with an inexplicit boss by initiating an ongoing series of informal discussions about "good management" and "our objectives." Still others find useful information more indirectly through those who used to work for the boss and through the formal planning systems in which the boss makes commitments to his or her own superior. Which approach you choose, of course, should depend on your understanding of your boss's style.

Developing a workable set of mutual expectations also requires that you communicate your own expectations to the boss, find out if they are realistic, and influence the boss to accept the ones that are important to you. Being able to influence the boss to value your expectations can be particularly important if the boss is an overachiever. Such a boss will often set unrealistically high standards that need to be brought into line with reality.

A flow of information
How much information a boss needs about what a subordinate is doing will vary significantly depending on the boss's style, the situation he or she is in, and the confidence the boss has in the subordinate. But it is not uncommon for a boss to need more information than the subordinate would naturally supply or for the subordinate to think the boss knows more than he or she really does. Effective managers recognize that they probably underestimate what their bosses need to know and make sure they find ways to keep them informed through processes that fit their styles.

Managing the flow of information upward is particularly difficult if the boss does not like to hear about problems. Although many people would deny it, bosses often give off signals that they want to hear only good news. They show great displeasure—usually nonverbally—when someone tells them about a problem. Ignoring individual achievement, they may even evaluate more favorably subordinates who do not bring problems to them.

Nevertheless, for the good of the organization, the boss, and the subordinate, a superior needs to hear about failures as well as successes. Some subordinates deal with a good-news-only boss by finding indirect ways to get the necessary information to him or her, such as a management information system. Others see to it that potential problems, whether in the form of good surprises or bad news, are communicated immediately.

Dependability and honesty

Few things are more disabling to a boss than a subordinate on whom he cannot depend, whose work he cannot trust. Almost no one is intentionally undependable, but many managers are inadvertently so because of oversight or uncertainty about the boss's priorities. A commitment to an optimistic delivery date may please a superior in the short term but become a source of displeasure if not honored. It's difficult for a boss to rely on a subordinate who repeatedly slips deadlines. As one president (describing a subordinate) put it: "I'd rather he be more consistent even if he delivered fewer peak successes—at least I could rely on him."

Nor are many managers intentionally dishonest with their bosses. But it is easy to shade the truth and play down issues. Current concerns often become future surprise problems. It's almost impossible for bosses to work effectively if they cannot rely on a fairly accurate reading from their subordinates. Because it undermines credibility, dishonesty is perhaps the most troubling trait a subordinate can have. Without a basic level of trust, a boss feels compelled to check all of a subordinate's decisions, which makes it difficult to delegate.

Good use of time and resources

Your boss is probably as limited in his or her store of time, energy, and influence as you are. Every request you make of your boss uses up some of these resources, so it's wise to draw on these resources selectively. This may sound obvious, but many managers use up their boss's time (and some of their own credibility) over relatively trivial issues.

One vice president went to great lengths to get his boss to fire a meddlesome secretary in another department. His boss had to use considerable influence to do it. Understandably, the head of the other department was not pleased. Later, when the vice president wanted to tackle more important problems, he ran into trouble. By using up blue chips on a relatively trivial issue, he had made it difficult for him and his boss to meet more important goals.

No doubt, some subordinates will resent that on top of all their other duties, they also need to take time and energy to manage their relationships with their bosses. Such managers fail to realize the importance of this activity and how it can simplify their jobs by eliminating potentially severe problems. Effective managers recognize that this part of their work is legitimate. Seeing themselves as ultimately responsible for what they achieve in an organization, they know they need to establish and manage relationships with everyone on whom they depend—and that includes the boss.

Originally published in January 1980. Reprint R0501J

Get the Boss to Buy In

by Susan J. Ashford and James Detert

AN ENGINEERING MANAGER at an energy company—we'll call him John Healy—wanted to sell his boss on a safer and cheaper gas-scrubbing technology. This might have been an easy task if his boss, the general manager, hadn't selected the existing system just a year before. Instead it was, in Healy's words, "a delicate process." Fortunately, user reviews of the new technology had become available only in the past several months, which Healy tactfully mentioned in his presentation to the GM and other senior executives. He also included a detailed comparison of the two systems, drawing on implementations at comparable plants; the data suggested that the new system would remove contaminants more efficiently and reduce costs by about $700,000 a year. Because the GM was still on the fence, Healy brought in a bio-gas expert his boss trusted and respected to talk about the new technology's merits. The company made the investment and adopted the new system.

Organizations don't prosper unless managers in the middle ranks, like Healy, identify and promote the need for change. People at that level gather valuable intelligence from direct contact with customers, suppliers, and colleagues. They're in a position to see when the market is ripe for a certain offering, for instance, or to detect early signs that a partnership won't work out. But for many reasons, ranging from a fear of negative consequences to compliance with a top-down culture, they may not voice their ideas and concerns. As we

Middle managers are more likely to speak up when they:

- Identify with the organization
- Have a positive relationship with their audience
- Feel psychologically safe in the organization
- Think someone above them will take action
- Care enough about the issue to invest energy in selling it

know from our research and others' work in this area, not to mention recent news stories, such silence can have dire consequences—like "regulatory capture" in banking and unchecked product safety risks.

Even when they do speak up, most managers struggle to sell their ideas to people at the top. They find it difficult to raise issues to a "strategic" level early in the decision-making process—if they gain entry into such conversations at all. Studies show that senior executives dismiss good ideas from below far too often, largely for this reason: If they don't already perceive an idea's relevance to organizational performance, they don't deem it important enough to merit their attention. Middle managers have to work to alter that perception.

Their task is easier if certain contextual factors are in place—for instance, a track record of strong individual contributions, which enhances credibility, and a culture in which it's safe to speak up. Whether or not those stars are aligned, managers can improve their odds of success by using powerful methods of persuasion. Consider John Healy's approach: He presented his idea with emotional intelligence (making sure the GM didn't look bad for buying the current system), supported it with strong evidence from similar companies, and brought in a carefully chosen outside expert to bolster his argument.

Since Jane Dutton and Susan Ashford (a coauthor of this article) introduced the concept of "issue selling" into the academic discourse, more than two decades ago, many studies have proposed tactics for effectively winning support for new ideas. In a recent study of our own, we examined what actually works in organizations,

Idea in Brief

The Problem

Middle managers glean valuable insights from their contact with customers, suppliers, and colleagues—but they struggle to sell their ideas to decision makers at the top. As a result, their organizations fail to seize opportunities and solve problems.

The Solution

Research shows that managers who gain buy-in from senior executives use seven tactics more often than managers whose ideas don't go anywhere.

The Benefits

These tactics provide a powerful framework for leading change from the middle ranks. By using them in an extended campaign for support, you can persuade senior leaders to take action and accomplish your goals.

across a range of roles and industries. Our participants described their experiences selling three basic types of ideas: new products, processes, markets, or customers to pursue; improvements to existing products or processes; and ways of better meeting employees' needs.

Issue sellers who accomplish their goals, we found, look for the best ways, venues, and times to voice their ideas and concerns—using rhetorical skill, political sensitivity, and interpersonal connections to move the right leaders to action. In particular, they employ seven tactics significantly more often than people who don't succeed in gaining buy-in. In this article we pull those tactics into a practical framework that managers can use to gain traction for their ideas, and we illustrate them with examples from our research. Each tactic should be part of an extended campaign to win attention and resources.

Tactic 1: Tailor Your Pitch

More than any other tactic in our research sample, tailoring the pitch to decision makers was associated with success. It's essential for issue sellers to familiarize themselves with their audience's unique blend of goals, values, and knowledge and to allow that insight to shape their messages.

That's how one regional sales manager in the Canada division of an international oil company persuaded senior executives to restructure the sales organization and change its approach to attracting and motivating talent. Although sales teams in the oil industry are usually organized by customer, at this company each one covered a region. Because many customers had offices in multiple regions, teams often undermined one another's efforts by offering competing deals to the same clients. The organization's poor structure led to misaligned incentives and a fragmented customer experience. Making matters worse, most of the reps worked for salaries rather than commissions. "That's why a competitor managed to poach more than half my division's sales force," the regional manager said. Unsurprisingly, nearly all the top performers had left. Having a sales structure so inefficient and out of touch with standard practices made such attrition practically inevitable. Although the executives who had created the structure were competent, they lacked sales experience. The remaining sales team, similarly, was technically knowledgeable but inexperienced, and the force was too small to sustain the business, let alone grow it.

When the regional manager initially shared his concerns with his boss and a few other executives, they disagreed, saying that the solution was simply to push people harder. "That sounded very risky to me, given that the division had just lost more than half its sales team," he told us. He made little progress until he asked other leaders in the division—those with greater decision-making power—what they expected from sales. He met with the new vice president of marketing and sales for Canada, for example, who wanted to prevent teams from working against one another and damaging credibility with clients.

In light of the feedback he'd gathered, the regional manager drafted recommendations and explained how they would help the division double revenue within four years (a target the CEO had recently announced to shareholders). Assigning sales teams to clients rather than to regions, he pointed out, would keep reps from stepping on one another's toes—which addressed the Canada VP's concerns. The manager also argued that attracting and retaining seasoned salespeople was essential to increasing revenue within the CEO's desired time frame. He emphasized the division's high attrition rate for reps—about 40% walked out the door each year—and described how that could be fixed by following the industry's best practices for recruiting and managing sales talent. Commission-based compensation would attract experienced people and give them a reason to stay. Training would help greener reps develop important skills for managing customer relationships.

The Canada VP approved the plan and, more important, provided the resources to carry it out. "We added a dozen experienced people to the sales organization," the regional manager said. "And after implementation we had only one person leave in four years." That reduced the once-sizable turnover costs to almost nothing. The division also invested $75,000 in training, which more than paid for itself with a contest to see who could sell the most using the methods learned. (That alone brought $2.7 million in new business in one week.) Although the division missed its four-year target, it doubled revenue in five years.

In light of those benefits, executives no longer blamed laziness for the problems the sales force had experienced. And good people stopped leaving in droves, thanks partly to the shift in mindset at the top and partly to the improved structure and talent practices.

The regional manager attributed the inroads he made to his carefully tailored pitch. In addition to speaking directly to the Canada VP's and other leaders' goals, he said, "I had to show how my ideas could help meet the CEO's revenue expectations." That allowed him to move from one-on-one and small group meetings to a written proposal and a presentation he could share at a more senior level, where the initiatives got the support they needed.

Tactic 2: Frame the Issue

An issue's place on your organization's list of priorities depends heavily on how you package the idea. A new technological development might seem like techie trivia until you explain how it supports a strategic goal, such as increasing responsiveness to customers. It then becomes important. Once people see how your initiative fits into the big picture, they'll be more willing to devote resources to it.

Similarly, if you're a unit head presenting one of your directors to top management for promotion, you'll want to say that she exceeded her targets and spell out how she can contribute to key goals. You can describe how moving her into a more strategic role will help turn around a struggling department, for instance, or bring energy and creativity to a modestly performing part of the business. By framing her as a leader the organization needs instead of simply letting her impressive work speak for itself, you create a sense of urgency for decision makers. This isn't just someone who has accomplished a lot and deserves to advance, whenever and however that's convenient. It's someone with the skills and drive to make changes that matter now.

As these scenarios show, it's often effective to highlight an idea's business benefits; the successful sellers in our research took that approach significantly more often than those who'd failed. For example, a chief investment officer at a financial firm described how he very gradually made the case that subscribing to a proprietary real estate database was "a need and not just a want." Every six months or so, over a period of about five years, he would float the suggestion at a moment when access to the database would be useful, and a tech-savvy ally in the asset management department would vocally agree. But they needed broader support for the idea, because most people viewed it as a luxury. "We are a lean-running organization that has historically resisted adopting new technologies," the chief investment officer explained. Eventually he identified a relevant need in another part of the business: The database could help the accounting department meet its public-reporting and audit requirements. That was the tipping point. He'd spelled out the business benefits for multiple departments. The firm decided to subscribe.

Moral framing appears to be less powerful than business framing. In our research, the few instances of moral framing were associated with failed attempts or uneven results. When issue sellers peddle

Issue-Selling Prompts

THESE QUESTIONS will help you use the seven tactics effectively:

Tailor Your Pitch

- Where does my audience stand on this issue?
- What does my audience find most convincing or compelling?

Frame the Issue

- How can I connect my issue to organizational priorities?
- How can I best describe its benefits?
- How can I link it to other issues receiving attention?
- How can I highlight an opportunity for the organization?

Manage Emotions on Both Sides

- How can I use my emotions to generate positive rather than negative responses?
- How can I manage my audience's emotional responses?

Get the Timing Right

- What is the best moment to be heard? Can I "catch the wave" of a trend, for example, or tap into what's going on in the outside world?
- What is the right time in the decision-making process to raise my issue?

Involve Others

- Which allies from my network can help me sell my issue, and how can I involve them effectively?
- Who are my potential blockers, and how can I persuade them to support me?
- Who are my fence-sitters, and how can I convince them that my issue matters?

Adhere to Norms

- Should I use a formal, public approach to sell my issue (for example, a presentation to upper management)? Or an informal, private approach (casual one-on-one conversations)? Or a combination of the two?

Suggest Solutions

- Am I suggesting a viable solution?
- If not, am I proposing a way to discover one instead of just highlighting the problem?

their principles too aggressively, people may react negatively to what they perceive as a judgment of their character.

Although focusing on business benefits is often safer, sellers may need to underscore the urgency. They might, for instance, present the idea as an opportunity that shouldn't be missed. Our successful sellers were significantly more likely than the others to explain what the organization stood to gain from their ideas. Emphasizing the positive can give your audience a sense of control over the situation and inspire optimism and buy-in.

Highlighting a threat—a consequence of not adopting your idea—can also create pressure to act. But it can backfire: When decision makers focus on potential loss, they sometimes then bury their heads and avoid the issue. The amount of threat framing did not differ between successful and unsuccessful selling attempts, perhaps because it was viewed as a mixed bag: It's hard to predict whether it will spur action—the classic "fight" response—or result in "flight."

Finally, issue sellers often find success by bundling their ideas with related ones. For instance, someone lobbying to increase leave time for employees caring for aging or sick family members might allude to efforts to increase parental leave. When attached to a larger initiative, a small idea can gain prominence. It's no longer just an elder-care issue; it's a work/life balance issue.

Tactic 3: Manage Emotions on Both Sides

Because issue selling is an interpersonal activity, often involving high stakes, it inevitably stirs emotions. Passion, if appropriately expressed, improves sellers' chances of gaining attention and triggering action. There's a fine line, however, between passion and anger. People sometimes propose initiatives because they are fed up with existing conditions or behavior. And as they encounter roadblocks to their selling efforts, their frustrations may intensify.

Though strong emotions can be channeled into a rousing appeal for action, when unregulated they're more likely to diminish the seller's influence. Decision makers who detect negative emotions from subordinates offering input tend to perceive those employees as complainers, not as change agents. Further, recent research by Wharton's Adam Grant shows that people who keep their emotions in check—or at least control what they display to others—feel more comfortable raising issues and receive higher performance evaluations.

Our study supports Grant's finding: Successful issue sellers paid much more attention to emotional regulation than those who failed. Indeed, the latter sometimes understood that their runaway emotions were partly to blame for their failures.

Important as self-regulation is, it's equally critical to understand and manage the decision maker's emotions—they, too, can make or break your case. John Healy, the manager in our opening example, did that especially well. Anticipating how his boss might feel about having selected the more hazardous and more expensive gas-scrubbing system, he was careful to point out that user reviews of the new technology hadn't been available when that decision had been made. Sellers hoping to have their issues heard should seek to inspire positive emotions in the decision makers—by focusing on benefits, for instance, or showing how action is possible. In our sample, successful sellers reported doing this far more often than others.

Tactic 4: Get the Timing Right

It's critical to find the right moment to raise your ideas. That moment might be when organizational priorities shift, when certain players leave or join the company, or when a boss's preoccupations change. Successful sellers in our study reported greater sensitivity than others to timing, by a wide margin. The best sellers notice when more and more people are beginning to care about a larger topic or trend that's related to their issue, and they position their idea to "catch the wave."

For example, the managing director of an Ecuadoran holding company's luxury division chose just the right time to persuade his CFO and board to tap an unexplored market in Peru. He'd gotten the idea in 2007. Though it was a viable option then, he held off on proposing it, given Peru's recent civil unrest and the fact that his division still had room for growth in its home market. In 2009, after the recession, "Peru had the best-performing stock market in the world," the director said. So his team took a trip to assess the potential. "We looked at new construction developments, and the modern minimalism was in stark contrast with the high-walled constructions from the guerrilla and terrorist era." It seemed that Peru was not just doing well but primed for growth. "There was only one prominent shopping mall, and 'hard' luxury items such as designer-branded bags, watches, and sunglasses were scarce or sold informally," he explained. "Yet Starbucks cafés were full every day and expanding." The director and his team decided that a luxury boutique carrying various products but focusing on watches would be the best project to pursue. They knew that department stores wouldn't cover the demand, because customers would want the luxury experience. "We thought Peru was ready for it," he said. The timing was excellent for another reason: The market in Ecuador had become saturated by then.

The director got the approval he needed, and the company opened two luxury stores in November 2010. "The day we opened our first boutique we sold the entire inventory of perfume we had bought from the pharmacy next door," he said. "One customer came in and bought all our stock of ink for his luxury writing instrument out of fear of not finding the ink again." That store accounted for 40% of the division's profits over the following three years. By 2011 all the most prestigious luxury brands had entered the Peruvian market—but this company had gotten there first.

In addition to keeping a close eye on larger trends and events, it's important to be mindful of deadlines. If an idea relates directly to an imminent product launch or software release, by all means speak up—now is the time to be heard. But as recent research shows, when a deadline is far away and decision makers are still in exploration mode, open-ended inquiry can be more effective than proposing a specific solution. Of course, sellers can't always know their audiences' deadlines. If you discover an immediate challenge, though, you can try to address it in your proposal—and shelve other ideas until people have time to really think them through.

Tactic 5: Involve Others

Issue sellers usually are better off bringing others into their efforts than going it alone. Building a coalition generates organizational buy-in more quickly and on a larger scale as more people contribute energy and resources. One person might have access to important data, for example, and another might have a personal relationship with one of the top managers you're trying to persuade. Perhaps recognizing these advantages, our successful respondents were more likely than the others to involve colleagues in pitching their ideas.

Negotiation experts would tell you to mobilize your allies, persuade your blockers to support the issue or at least back off, and show the fence-sitters why they should care about your idea. When building a coalition, you can reach out to experts in relevant areas to add to your credibility, though a recent study of reactions to issue sellers suggests that it's just as important to include individuals the target audience trusts. Certainly tap members of your network, but also involve people whose networks don't overlap with yours. That will expand the pool of people who might advocate for your idea or lend their expertise.

Tactic 6: Adhere to Norms

The tactics we've covered so far draw on two types of knowledge that successful issue sellers need: strategic (understanding the organization's goals, the plans to achieve them, and the roles decision makers play in those efforts) and relational (figuring out who will be affected by your issue, who cares about it, who might object to it, and so on). Here we'll discuss a third type: knowledge of organizational norms, such as what kinds of data your leaders like to use to make decisions, how they prefer to receive information, and whether they tend to get behind issues similar to yours. Grasping such norms can give you a sense of how effective the other tactics described in this article will be. For example, a study of employees selling environmental issues found that the use of drama and emotion worked only if the organization already had a strong environmental commitment.

One important norm to understand is whether it's generally best to use formal or informal approaches. Casual conversations allow issue sellers to get an off-the-record read on their ideas and avoid putting their target audience on the spot in public. But formal approaches can convey seriousness and apply helpful pressure on decision makers to respond. Issue sellers need to consider these trade-offs in light of what's expected in their organizations. In one company we studied, senior managers claimed to want innovative thinking but were described, even at "blue sky" meetings, as chastising those who didn't present slide shows using company-approved templates. Not surprisingly, their employees reported selling in very formal ways while acknowledging the dampening effect this probably had on innovation.

Successful sellers used more formal—and fewer informal—tactics than those whose pitches failed. So it seems that many business settings require a certain level of convention and decorum, and that the best sellers adapt their behavior to fit that norm. Our qualitative data suggests that sequencing matters, though: People who succeeded tended to roll out their ideas informally early on, in order to gauge interest, and then switch to formal presentations.

Tactic 7: Suggest Solutions

Clearly, people believe that if they're going to speak up about problems, they'd better suggest thoughtful fixes: This was the most frequently used tactic among both types of sellers, successful and not. And those who succeeded used it significantly more often than those who didn't. They pointed to specific solutions, such as adding a business operations team to address a systems flaw. They often included funding ideas when selling the need for something new.

Proposing a solution signals that the seller has put thought into the issue and respects leaders' time. Indeed, recent laboratory research shows that people think more highly of issue sellers who suggest solutions.

But here's the hitch: If people are less likely to raise issues for which they haven't identified a solution, as our data shows, organizations where problems crop up faster than people can devise fixes are at a considerable disadvantage. What's more, some problems are best solved by a group of people who bring diverse knowledge, experience, and expertise to the table. In these cases, expecting issue sellers to have solutions in hand may lead to poor decision-making.

Sellers who feel strongly about an issue but don't see a solution can suggest a sensible process for discovering one. That way they follow the norm of being solution-focused while getting others constructively involved in a timely manner.

Create a Tactical Campaign

There's more to a pitch than a big presentation and a yea-or-nay decision. Those are just the most visible steps in the process. Leading up to them, you should carefully lay a foundation for your argument, tactic by tactic, as you acquire resources and knowledge. Here are some principles to help you make the most of the tactics we've described.

Choose your battles

Some ideas are just plain tough to sell—those that are too far ahead of the audience's current understanding, for instance, or too much of a stretch beyond the organization's norms. That's especially true of any idea that may seem an indictment of the status quo or, worse, of the audience's intelligence, judgment, or morality. In such cases, you may have an uphill battle no matter how skillfully you frame the issue and manage emotions.

Even the best issue sellers can't win every time, and sometimes the payoff isn't worth the effort. To determine whether to invest resources and social capital in selling an issue, ask two questions: How important is this to my company? And how important is it to me? That will help you assess how much risk to take on. Raising concerns about a company's approach to foreign labor practices or about managers' treatment of employees will probably elicit much

About the Research

WE SURVEYED 77 men and 24 women, ages 24 to 52, and, with the help of research assistant Evan Bruno, interviewed 10 of them. Our respondents had 14 years of work experience, on average—about six years in their organizations and about two and a half in their current roles. They held a variety of jobs, from business analyst to director of marketing to principal engineer, and worked in industries ranging from software development to consumer goods to law.

About half the respondents (randomly selected) were asked to describe a time when they successfully pitched an idea to decision makers; the other half, a time when they failed. All indicated how they knew that their efforts had succeeded or failed and rated the extent to which they'd used each of the tactics in this article. We examined whether each tactic appeared more frequently in the success stories than in the failure stories, testing for statistically significant differences between the two groups. We also identified which tactics played the largest role in each success or failure.

more pushback than ideas for enhancing products or improving processes. But if the former issues are critical to the organization's well-being or your own professional identity, you might sensitively pursue them even if you know you won't succeed in the short term.

Combine tactics

In our regression analysis, we found that campaigns using multiple tactics succeeded more often than those using any single tactic. Indeed, the combined use of all seven tactics accounted for about 40% of the difference between successes and failures. We saw the same kind of impact in individuals' descriptions of their selling efforts. The engineering manager at the energy company managed the GM's emotions, suggested a solution backed by data, and turned to an outside expert for further support. The Ecuadoran managing director also combined tactics: In addition to choosing the right moment to launch the luxury goods stores, he adhered to his conservative organization's norms for proposing projects—starting with informal conversations, looking at proxy businesses in other industries (in this case, Starbucks), talking with customers and partners to gather insights, and finally building up to the formal review process, using traditional financial tools and outsourced market studies for analysis.

Approach the right audience

It's a common dilemma: Should you air your idea with your boss and risk getting nowhere because he or she lacks sufficient power or interest to back you up? Or go straight to decision makers who will care—and quite likely pay a price for bypassing your manager? Wishing to avoid trouble, many sellers start with their boss and hope their ideas make their way up the hierarchy. But their issues often die right away or languish until senior management becomes aware of them. Sometimes the immediate boss doesn't even bother escalating the issue; other times the messenger isn't as skilled as the initial seller at making the case.

So ask if you can accompany anyone selling on your behalf, whether that's your manager or a colleague who has an "in" with a formal decision-making body. If that's not possible, do everything you can to prepare that person to sell effectively: Work out the details of the business case, help identify the right time and venue for presenting it, and so forth. If you decide to approach decision makers directly, keep your boss in the loop. Otherwise you'll need to have a very good answer when senior leaders ask why you've come to them instead of to your manager.

No set of prescriptions can capture the nuances of every environment or remove the risks and disappointments of issue selling. But sellers who routinely and effectively use these tactics enjoy greater success than those who don't.

Issue selling isn't a discrete event; it's an ongoing process that requires groundwork, pacing, and patience. When mid-level managers do it effectively, their ideas get decision makers' attention and make a real difference.

Originally published in January–February 2015. Reprint R1501E

The Secrets of Great Teamwork

by Martine Haas and Mark Mortensen

TODAY'S TEAMS ARE DIFFERENT from the teams of the past: They're far more diverse, dispersed, digital, and dynamic (with frequent changes in membership). But while teams face new hurdles, their success still hinges on a core set of fundamentals for group collaboration.

The basics of team effectiveness were identified by J. Richard Hackman, a pioneer in the field of organizational behavior who began studying teams in the 1970s. In more than 40 years of research, he uncovered a groundbreaking insight: What matters most to collaboration is not the personalities, attitudes, or behavioral styles of team members. Instead, what teams need to thrive are certain "enabling conditions." In our own studies (see the sidebar "About the Research"), we've found that three of Hackman's conditions—a compelling direction, a strong structure, and a supportive context—continue to be particularly critical to team success. In fact, today those three requirements demand more attention than ever. But we've also seen that modern teams are vulnerable to two corrosive problems—"us versus them" thinking and incomplete information. Overcoming those pitfalls requires a fourth critical condition: a shared mindset.

The key takeaway for leaders is this: Though teams face an increasingly complicated set of challenges, a relatively small number of factors have an outsized impact on their success. Managers

About the Research

OVER THE PAST 15 years, we've studied teams and groups in a variety of contemporary settings. We've conducted nine large research projects in global organizations, undertaking more than 300 interviews and 4,200 surveys with team leaders and managers. The teams involved worked on projects in product development, sales, operations, finance, R&D, senior management, and more, in a wide range of industries, including software, professional services, manufacturing, natural resources, and consumer products. In addition, we have conducted executive education sessions on team effectiveness for thousands of team leaders and members; their stories and experiences have also shaped our thinking.

can achieve big returns if they understand what those factors are and focus on getting them right.

The Enabling Conditions

Let's explore in greater detail how to create a climate that helps diverse, dispersed, digital, dynamic teams—what we like to call 4-D teams—attain high performance.

Compelling direction

The foundation of every great team is a direction that energizes, orients, and engages its members. Teams cannot be inspired if they don't know what they're working toward and don't have explicit goals. Those goals should be challenging (modest ones don't motivate) but not so difficult that the team becomes dispirited. They also must be consequential: People have to care about achieving a goal, whether because they stand to gain extrinsic rewards, like recognition, pay, and promotions; or intrinsic rewards, such as satisfaction and a sense of meaning.

On 4-D teams, direction is especially crucial because it's easy for far-flung members from dissimilar backgrounds to hold different views of the group's purpose. Consider one global team we studied. All the members agreed that serving their client was their goal, but what that meant varied across locations. Members in Norway equated it with providing a product of the absolute highest

Idea in Brief

The Problem

Teams are more diverse, dispersed, digital, and dynamic than ever before. These qualities make collaboration especially challenging.

The Analysis

Mixing new insights with a focus on the fundamentals of team effectiveness identified by organizational-behavior pioneer J. Richard Hackman, managers should work to establish the conditions that will enable teams to thrive.

The Solution

The right conditions are:

- a compelling direction
- a strong structure
- a supportive context, and
- a shared mindset

Weaknesses in these areas make teams vulnerable to problems.

quality—no matter what the cost. Their colleagues in the UK, however, felt that if the client needed a solution that was only 75% accurate, the less precise solution would better serve that client. Solving this tension required a frank discussion to reach consensus on how the team as a whole defined its objectives.

Strong structure

Teams also need the right mix and number of members, optimally designed tasks and processes, and norms that discourage destructive behavior and promote positive dynamics.

High-performing teams include members with a balance of skills. Every individual doesn't have to possess superlative technical and social skills, but the team overall needs a healthy dose of both. Diversity in knowledge, views, and perspectives, as well as in age, gender, and race, can help teams be more creative and avoid groupthink.

This is one area where 4-D teams often have an advantage. In research we conducted at the World Bank, we found that teams benefited from having a blend of cosmopolitan and local members—that is, people who have lived in multiple countries and speak multiple languages, and people with deep roots in the area they're working in. Cosmopolitan members bring technical knowledge and skills and expertise that apply in many situations, while locals bring country knowledge and insight into an area's politics, culture, and tastes. In one of the bank's teams, this combination proved critical to the success of a project upgrading an urban slum in West Africa. A local member pointed out that a microcredit scheme might be necessary to help residents pay for the new water and sanitation services planned by the team, while a cosmopolitan member shared valuable information about problems faced in trying to implement such programs in other countries. Taking both perspectives into account, the team came up with a more sustainable design for its project.

Adding members is of course one way to ensure that a team has the requisite skills and diversity, but increased size comes with costs. Larger teams are more vulnerable to poor communication, fragmentation, and free riding (due to a lack of accountability). In the executive sessions we lead, we frequently hear managers lament that teams become bloated as global experts are pulled in and more members are recruited to increase buy-in from different locations, divisions, or functions. Team leaders must be vigilant about adding members only when necessary. The aim should be to include the minimum number—and no more. One manager told us that any time she receives a request to add a team member, she asks what unique value that person will bring to the group and, in cases where the team is already at capacity, which current member will be released.

Team assignments should be designed with equal care. Not every task has to be highly creative or inspiring; many require a certain amount of drudgery. But leaders can make any task more motivating by ensuring that the team is responsible for a significant piece of work from beginning to end, that the team members have a lot of autonomy in managing that work, and that the team receives performance feedback on it.

With 4-D teams, people in different locations often handle different components of a task, which raises challenges. Consider a software design team based in Santa Clara, California, that sends chunks of code to its counterparts in Bangalore, India, to revise overnight. Such 24/7 development is common as firms seek to use time zone differences to their advantage. But in one such team we spoke with, that division of labor was demotivating, because it left the Indian team members with a poor sense of how the pieces of code fit together and with little control over what they did and how. Moreover, the developers in Bangalore got feedback only when what they sent back didn't fit. Repartitioning the work to give them ownership over an entire module dramatically increased their motivation and engagement and improved the quality, quantity, and efficiency of their work.

Destructive dynamics can also undermine collaborative efforts. We've all seen team members withhold information, pressure people to conform, avoid responsibility, cast blame, and so on. Teams can reduce the potential for dysfunction by establishing clear norms— rules that spell out a small number of things members must always do (such as arrive at meetings on time and give everyone a turn to speak) and a small number they must never do (such as interrupt). Instilling such norms is especially important when team members operate across different national, regional, or organizational cultures (and may not share the same view of, for example, the importance of punctuality). And in teams whose membership is fluid, explicitly reiterating norms at regular intervals is key.

Supportive context

Having the right support is the third condition that enables team effectiveness. This includes maintaining a reward system that reinforces good performance, an information system that provides access to the data needed for the work, and an educational system that offers training, and last—but not least—securing the material resources required to do the job, such as funding and technological assistance. While no team ever gets everything it wants, leaders can head off a lot of problems by taking the time to get the essential pieces in place from the start.

Ensuring a supportive context is often difficult for teams that are geographically distributed and digitally dependent, because the resources available to members may vary a lot. Consider the experience of Jim, who led a new product-development team at General Mills that focused on consumer goods for the Mexican market. While Jim was based in the United States, in Minnesota, some members of his team were part of a wholly owned subsidiary in Mexico. The team struggled to meet its deadlines, which caused friction. But when Jim had the opportunity to visit his Mexican team members, he realized how poor their IT was and how strapped they were for both capital and people—particularly in comparison with the headquarters staff. In that one visit Jim's frustration turned to admiration for how much his Mexican colleagues were able to accomplish with so little, and he realized that the problems he'd assumed were due to a clash between cultures were actually the result of differences in resources.

Shared mindset

Establishing the first three enabling conditions will pave the way for team success, as Hackman and his colleagues showed. But our research indicates that today's teams need something more. Distance and diversity, as well as digital communication and changing membership, make them especially prone to the problems of "us versus them" thinking and incomplete information. The solution to both is developing a shared mindset among team members—something team leaders can do by fostering a common identity and common understanding.

In the past teams typically consisted of a stable set of fairly homogeneous members who worked face-to-face and tended to have a similar mindset. But that's no longer the case, and teams now often perceive themselves not as one cohesive group but as several smaller subgroups. This is a natural human response: Our brains use cognitive shortcuts to make sense of our increasingly complicated world, and one way to deal with the complexity of a 4-D team is to lump people into categories. But we also are inclined to view our own subgroup—whether it's our function, our unit, our region, or our culture—more positively than others, and that habit often creates tension and hinders collaboration.

This was the challenge facing Alec, the manager of an engineering team at ITT tasked with providing software solutions for high-end radio communications. His team was split between Texas and New Jersey, and the two groups viewed each other with skepticism and apprehension. Differing time zones, regional cultures, and even accents all reinforced their dissimilarities, and Alec struggled to keep all members up to speed on strategies, priorities, and roles. The situation got so bad that during a team visit to a customer, members from the two offices even opted to stay in separate hotels. In an effort to unite the team, Alec took everyone out to dinner, only to find the two groups sitting at opposite ends of the table.

Incomplete information is likewise more prevalent in 4-D teams. Very often, certain team members have important information that others do not, because they are experts in specialized areas or because members are geographically dispersed, new, or both. That information won't provide much value if it isn't communicated to the rest of the team. After all, shared knowledge is the cornerstone of effective collaboration; it gives a group a frame of reference, allows the group to interpret situations and decisions correctly, helps people understand one another better, and greatly increases efficiency.

Digital dependence often impedes information exchange, however. In face-to-face teams, participants can rely on nonverbal and contextual cues to provide insight into what's going on. When we walk into an in-person meeting, for example, we can immediately sense the individual and collective moods of the people in the room—information that we use (consciously or not) to tailor subsequent interactions. Having to rely on digital communication erodes the transmission of this crucial type of intelligence.

Some effects of incomplete information came to light during a recent executive education session at Takeda Pharmaceuticals in Japan. The audience was split roughly 50/50 between employees based in Japan and those based in the United States. One of the U.S. managers took the opportunity to ask about something that had puzzled him. Takeda's "share the pain" strategy for dealing with time zone differences alternated the scheduling of conference calls between late nights in America and late nights in Asia, and he wondered why his Japanese colleagues seemed to take their late-night calls in the office, while he and his U.S. colleagues always took them at home. His Japanese colleagues' responses revealed a variety of motivations for this choice—desire for work/life separation, a need to run language questions by coworkers, and the lack of home office space in a typical Osaka apartment. But the result was the same: Though Takeda executives had intended to "share the pain," they had not. The Americans left the office at a normal hour, had dinner with their families, and held calls in the comfort of their homes, while their Japanese colleagues stayed in the office, missed time with their families, and hoped calls ended before the last train home. In this case, however, the incomplete information wasn't about the task; it was about something equally critical: how the Japanese members of the team experienced their work and their relationships with distant team members.

Fortunately, there are many ways team leaders can actively foster a shared identity and shared understanding and break down the barriers to cooperation and information exchange. One powerful approach is to ensure that each subgroup feels valued for its contributions toward the team's overall goals.

Returning to Alec, the manager of the team whose subgroups booked separate hotels: While his dinner started with the Texas colleagues at one end of the table and the New Jersey colleagues at the other, by its close signs had emerged that the team was chipping away at its internal wall. Over the following weeks, Alec stressed the important roles members from the two offices played in achieving the team's exciting and engaging goal—designing new software for remotely monitoring hardware. He emphasized that both subteams contributed necessary skills and pointed out that they depended on each other for success. To build more bridges, he brought the whole team together several more times over the next few months, creating shared experiences and common reference points and stories. Because of his persistent efforts, team members started to view the team not as "us and them" but as "we."

Many participants in our field research and executive education sessions promote shared understanding through a practice called "structured unstructured time"—that is, time blocked off in the schedule to talk about matters not directly related to the task at hand. Often this is done by reserving the first 10 minutes of teamwide meetings for open discussion. The idea is to provide an opportunity for members to converse about whatever aspects of work or daily life they choose, such as office politics or family or personal events. This helps people develop a more complete picture of distant colleagues, their work, and their environment. However, team leaders must make the discussion's purpose and norms clear or else face 10 minutes of awkwardness as everyone waits for someone to speak.

One team we came across had a related tactic: Its members initially "met" over desktop video and gave one another virtual tours of their workspaces. By simply panning the camera around the room, they were able to show their remote colleagues their work environment—including things that were likely to distract or disrupt them, such as closely seated coworkers in an open-plan space or a nearby photocopier. After the tours the team members found that they were better able to interpret and understand distant colleagues' attitudes and behaviors.

Evaluating Your Team

Together the four enabling conditions form a recipe for building an effective team from scratch. But even if you inherit an existing team, you can set the stage for its success by focusing on the four fundamentals.

How will you know if your efforts are working? Hackman proposed evaluating team effectiveness on three criteria: output, collaborative ability, and members' individual development. We have found that these criteria apply as well as ever and advise that leaders use them to calibrate their teams over time. The ideal approach combines regular light-touch monitoring for preventive maintenance and less frequent but deeper checks when problems arise.

For ongoing monitoring, we recommend a simple and quick temperature check: Every few months, rate your team on each of the four enabling conditions and also on the three criteria of team effectiveness. (See the sidebar "Does Your Team Measure Up?".) Look in particular at the lowest-scored condition and

Does Your Team Measure Up?

TO SEE HOW YOUR TEAM is doing, evaluate it on the three classic criteria of team effectiveness. Then look at how well it meets the four conditions that drive the success of teams in a diverse, dispersed, digital, dynamic business. Underperformance on the criteria and weaknesses in the conditions are usually linked. Understanding the connections between them can help your team identify ways to improve.

On a scale of 1 (worst) to 5 (best), rate your team on these criteria:

Output	Collaborative ability	Individual development
Are our customers happy with our output—with its quality, quantity, and delivery?	Do our team's dynamics help us work well together?	Are individual team members improving their knowledge, skills, and abilities?

Then score your team on the following aspects of the conditions for effectiveness:

Compelling direction	Strong structure	Supportive context	Shared mindset
Do we have a common goal that is clear, challenging (but not impossible), and consequential?	Do we have the right number and mix of members? Are people responsible for tasks from beginning to end? Do we have clear norms for acceptable conduct?	Do we have the resources, information, and training we need? Are there appropriate rewards for success?	Do the team members have a strong common identity? Do we readily share information with one another and understand one another's constraints and context?

This assessment draws on the seminal research of the organizational-behavior expert J. Richard Hackman. You can find more of his insights in *Leading Teams: Setting the Stage for Great Performance* (Harvard Business School Publishing, 2002).

lowest-scored effectiveness criteria, and consider how they're connected. The results will show where your team is on track as well as where problems may be brewing.

If you need a deeper diagnosis—perhaps in the face of poor performance or a crisis—block out an hour or more to conduct an intervention assessment. Carefully examine the links between the lowest-rated conditions and team effectiveness criteria; managers who do this usually discover clear relationships between them, which suggest a path forward.

You can conduct both the quick check and the deeper intervention on your own or assess overall alignment by having all team members assign ratings separately. For a team-based check, you should compare results across the group. For a team-based intervention, you can increase the impact by holding a full-scale workshop, where all the members get together to discuss and compare results. Not only does this give you more-complete data—shining a light on potential blind spots—but it also reveals differences among viewpoints and opens up areas for discussion. We have found that it is frequently through the process of comparing assessments—a leader's with the team's, and the team members' with their peers'—that the deepest insights arise.

Teamwork has never been easy—but in recent years it has become much more complex. And the trends that make it more difficult seem likely to continue, as teams become increasingly global, virtual, and project-driven. Taking a systematic approach to analyzing how well your team is set up to succeed—and identifying where improvements are needed—can make all the difference.

Originally published in June 2016. Reprint R1606E

How the Best Bosses Interrupt Bias on Their Teams

by Joan C. Williams and Sky Mihaylo

COMPANIES SPEND MILLIONS on antibias training each year. The goal is to create workforces that are more inclusive, and thereby more innovative and more effective. Studies show that well-managed diverse groups outperform homogeneous ones and are more committed, have higher collective intelligence, and are better at making decisions and solving problems. But research also shows that bias prevention programs rarely deliver. And some companies don't invest in them at all. So how can you, as an individual leader, make sure your team is including and making the most of diverse voices? Can one person fix what an entire organization can't?

Although bias itself is devilishly hard to eliminate, it is not as difficult to *interrupt*. In the decades we've spent researching and advising people on how to build and manage diverse work groups, we've identified ways that managers can counter bias without spending a lot of time—or political capital.

The first step is to understand the four distinct ways bias plays out in everyday work interactions: (1) *Prove it again:* Some groups have to prove themselves more than others do. (2) *Tightrope:* A narrower range of behaviors is accepted from some groups than from others. (3) *Maternal wall:* Women with children see their commitment and competence questioned or face disapproval for being too career focused. (4) *Tug-of-war:* Disadvantaged groups find themselves pitted against one another because of differing strategies for assimilating—or refusing to do so.

The second step is to recognize when and where these forms of bias arise day-to-day. In the absence of an organizational directive, it's easy to let them go unaddressed. That's a mistake. You can't be a great manager without becoming a *bias interrupter*. Here's how to do it.

Picking Your People

Bias in hiring has been extensively documented. In one study, "Jamal" needed eight more years of experience than "Greg" to be seen as equally qualified. Another found that men from elite backgrounds were called back for interviews more than 12 times as often as identical candidates from non-elite backgrounds. Other studies have found that women, LGBT+ candidates, people with disabilities, women in headscarves, and older people are less likely to be hired than their peers.

Fairness in hiring is only the first step toward achieving diversity, but it's an important one. Here are four simple actions that will yield the best candidates by eliminating artificial advantages:

1. Insist on a diverse pool

Whether you're working with recruiters or doing the hiring yourself, make it clear from the outset that you want true diversity, not just one female or minority candidate. Research shows that the odds of hiring a woman are 79 times as great if at least two women are in the finalist pool, while the odds of hiring a nonwhite candidate are 194 times as great with at least two finalist minority applicants. For example, when Kori Carew launched the Shook Scholars Institute at Shook, Hardy & Bacon, she designed it to bring a diverse mix of students into the law firm and offered career development and mentoring that prompted many of them to apply for summer associate positions.

2. Establish objective criteria, define "culture fit," and demand accountability

Implicit biases around culture fit often lead to homogeneity. Too often it comes down to shared backgrounds and interests that

Idea in Brief

Companies spend millions on antibias training each year in hopes of creating more-inclusive—and thereby innovative and effective—workforces. Studies show that well-managed diverse groups perform better and are more committed, have higher collective intelligence, and excel at making decisions and solving problems. But research also shows that bias-prevention programs rarely deliver. So what can you, as an individual leader, do to ensure that your team is including and making the most of diverse voices? How can one person fix what an entire organization can't?

Although bias itself is devilishly hard to change, it is not as difficult to interrupt. The authors have identified several practices that managers can use to counter bias (and avoid its negative effects) without spending a lot of time or political capital. In hiring, leaders should insist on a diverse pool, precommit to objective criteria, limit referral hiring, and structure interviews around skills-based questions. Day to day, they should ensure that high- and low-value work is assigned evenly and run meetings in a way that guarantees all voices are heard. In evaluating and developing people, they should clarify criteria for positive reviews and promotions, stick to those rules, and separate potential from performance and personality from skill sets.

out-groups, especially first-generation professionals, won't have. That's why it's important to clarify objective criteria for any open role and to rate all applicants using the same rubric. When one insurance company began hiring in this way, it ended up offering jobs to 46% more minority candidates than before. Even if your organization doesn't mandate this approach, ensure that everyone on your team takes it. Write down the specific qualifications required for a particular position so that everyone can focus on them when reviewing résumés and conducting interviews. For example, when Alicia Powell was managing chief counsel at PNC Bank, she made a point of listing the qualities that would make new team members successful in their roles: proactive in managing risk, self-disciplined, patient, customer focused, and independent. Powell shared this information with the rest of her team and candidates, ensuring that everyone was on the same page. You should hold people accountable in the same way. Waive criteria rarely, and require an explanation for those exceptions; then keep track of long-term waiving trends. Research shows that objective rules tend to be applied rigorously to out-groups but leniently to in-groups.

3. Limit referral hiring

If your organization is homogeneous, hiring from within or from employees' social networks will only perpetuate that. So reach out to women and minority groups. Google partners with historically Black colleges such as Spelman and Florida A&M University and with Hispanic-serving institutions such as New Mexico State and the University of Puerto Rico, Mayagüez. As an individual leader, you can work with the same organizations or recruit from similar ones in your industry or local community.

4. Structure interviews with skills-based questions

Ask every person interviewed the same questions and make sure that each question directly relates to the desired knowledge and skills you've outlined. Rate the answers immediately—that will allow you to compare candidates fairly on a preestablished rubric and prevent favoritism. You should also use skills assessments: Rather than ask "How comfortable are you with Excel?" say "Here's a data set. How would you find out X?" For more-complex skills, such as project management, pose a problem or a task that candidates are likely to encounter on the job and ask them to describe in detail how they would handle it.

Managing Day-to-Day

Even good leaders sometimes fall into bad habits when it comes to the daily management of their teams. Women report doing about 20% more "office housework," on average, than their white male counterparts, whether it's literal housework (arranging for lunch or cleaning up after a meeting), administrative tasks (finding a place to meet or prepping a PowerPoint), emotional labor ("He's upset—can you fix it?"), or undervalued work (mentoring summer interns). This is especially true in high-status, high-stakes workplaces. Women engineers report a "worker bee" expectation at higher rates than white men do, and women of color report it at higher rates than white women do. Meanwhile, glamour work that leads to networking and promotion opportunities, such as project leadership and presentations, goes disproportionately to white men. When the consultancy GapJumpers analyzed the performance reviews of a tech company client, it found that women employees were 42% more likely than their male colleagues to be limited to lower-impact projects; as a result, far fewer of them rose to more-senior roles.

Meetings are another problem area. Research shows that men are more likely than women to dominate the conversation, and that whereas men with expertise tend to be *more* influential, women with expertise tend to be *less* so. Our study of lawyers found that half of women report being interrupted in meetings at a higher rate than their male peers are. Another study found that in meetings that included more men than women (a common scenario), women typically participated about 25% less often than their male coworkers did. Double standards and stereotypes play out whenever diverse identities come together. Is a woman "emotional," or a Black man "angry," while a white male is "passionate"? We once heard from a woman scientist that she was sharply criticized as "aggressive" when she brought up a flaw in a male colleague's analysis; after that she felt she needed to just "bring in baked goods and be agreeable." A Black tech company executive we know told us about a meeting during which she said little while the only other woman, an Asian-American, said a lot. But she later heard that people thought she had "dominated" the conversation while her Asian-American peer had been "very quiet."

Unsure whether this sort of thing is happening on your team? Start tracking assignments and airtime in meetings. Use our free online tools (at http://bias interrupters.org/toolkits/orgtools/) to find out which work done by your group is higher- or lower-profile and who's doing what. For meetings, pay attention: Who's at the table? Who's doing the talking? Is someone taking notes when he or she could be leading the conversation? If you find a problematic dynamic, here are some ways to change it:

1. Set up a rotation for office housework, and don't ask for volunteers

"I always give these tasks to women because they do them well/volunteer" is a common refrain. This dynamic reflects an environment in which men suffer few consequences for bypassing or doing a poor job on low-value work, while women who do the same are seen as "prima donnas" or incompetent. Particularly when administrative staff is limited, a rotation helps level the playing field and makes it clear that everyone is expected to contribute to office housework. If you ask for volunteers, women and people of color will feel powerful pressure to prove they are "team players" by raising their hands.

2. Mindfully design and assign people to high-value projects

Sometimes we hear "It's true, I keep giving the plum assignments to a small group—but they're the only ones with the skills to do them!" According to Joyce Norcini, formerly general counsel for Nokia Siemens Networks, if you have only a tight circle of people you trust to handle meaningful work, you're in trouble. Her advice: Reconsider who is capable of doing what these important jobs require; chances are someone not on your usual list is. You may need to move outside your comfort zone and be more involved in the beginning, but having a broader range of trained people will serve you well in the end.

3. Acknowledge the importance of lower-profile contributions

"Diversity" hires may lag behind their majority-member peers because they're doing extra stuff that doesn't get them extra credit. If your organization truly prioritizes inclusion, then walk your talk. Many bosses who say they value diversity programming and mentorship don't actually take it into account when promotion or comp time becomes available. Integrating these contributions into individual goal setting and evaluating them during performance reviews is a simple start. And don't be afraid to think big: A law partner we know did such a great job running the woman's initiative that the firm begged her to stay on for another year. She said she would if the firm's bosses made her an equity partner. They did.

4. Respond to double standards, stereotyping, "manterruption," "bropriating," and "whipeating"

Pay close attention to the way people on your team talk about their peers and how they behave in group settings. For example, men tend to interrupt women far more often than the other way around; displays of confidence and directness *decrease* women's influence but *increase* men's. If a few people are dominating the conversation in a meeting, address it directly. Create and enforce a policy for interruptions. Keep track of those who drown others out and talk with them privately about it, explaining that you think it's important to hear everyone's contributions. Similarly, when you see instances of "bropriating" or "whipeating"—that is, majority-group members taking or being given credit for ideas that women and people of color originally offered—call it out. We know two women on the board of directors of a public company who made a pact: When a man tried to claim one of their ideas, the other would say something like "Yes, I liked Sandra's point, and I'm glad you did too." Once they did this consistently, bropriating stopped.

5. Ask people to weigh in

Women, people of Asian descent, and first-generation professionals report being brought up with a "modesty mandate" that can lead them to hold back their thoughts or speak in a tentative, deferential way. Counter this by extending an invitation: "Camilla, you have experience with this—what are we missing? Is this the best course of action?"

6. Schedule meetings inclusively

Business meetings should take place in the office, not at a golf course, a university club, or your favorite concert venue. Otherwise you're giving an artificial advantage to people who feel more comfortable in those settings or whose personal interests overlap with yours. Whenever possible, stick to working hours, or you risk putting caregivers and others with a demanding personal life at a disadvantage. Joan once noticed that no mothers were participating in a faculty appointment process because all the meetings were held at 5:30 PM. When she pointed this out to the person leading them, the problem was fixed immediately. This colleague had a stay-at-home wife and simply hadn't thought about the issue before.

7. Equalize access proactively

Bosses may meet with some employees more regularly than others, but it's important to make sure this is driven by business demands and team needs rather than by what individuals want or expect. White men may feel more comfortable walking into your office or asking for time. The same may be true of people whose interests you share. When Emily Gould Sullivan, who has led the employment law functions for two *Fortune* 500 retail companies, realized that she was routinely accepting "walking meeting" invitations from a team member who was, like her, interested in fitness, she made a point of reaching out to others to equalize access.

Developing Your Team

Your job as a manager is not only to get the best performance out of your team but also to encourage the development of each member. That means giving fair performance reviews, equal access to high-potential assignments, and promotions and pay increases to those who have earned them. Unfortunately, as we've noted, some groups need to prove themselves more than others, and a broader range of behaviors is often accepted from white men. For example, our research shows that assertiveness and anger are less likely to be accepted from people of color, and expectations that women will be modest, self-effacing, and nice often affect performance assessments. One study found that 66% of women's reviews contained comments about their personalities, but only 1% of men's reviews did. These double standards can have a real impact on equity outcomes. PayScale found that men of color were 25% less likely than their white peers to get a raise when they asked for one. And gender norms stunt careers for women. PayScale found that when women and men start their careers on the same rung of the professional ladder, by the time they are halfway (aged 30–44), 47% of men are managers or higher, but only 40% of women are. These numbers just worsen over time: Only 3% of the women make it to the C-suite, compared with 8% of the men.

Take these steps to avoid common pitfalls in evaluations and promotions:

1. Clarify evaluation criteria and focus on performance, not potential

Don't arrive at a rating without thinking about what predetermined benchmarks you've used to get there. Any evaluation should include enough data for a third party to understand the justification for the rating. Be specific. Instead of "She writes well," say "She can write an effective summary judgment motion under a tight deadline."

2. Separate performance from potential and personality from skill sets

In-groups tend to be judged on their potential and given the benefit of the doubt, whereas out-groups have to show they've nailed it. If your company values potential, it should be assessed separately, with factors clearly outlined for evaluators and employees. Then track whether there's a pattern as to who has "potential." If so, try relying on performance alone for everyone or get even more concrete with what you're measuring. Personality comments are no different; be wary of double standards that affect women and people of color when it comes to showing emotion or being congenial. Policing women into femininity doesn't help anyone, and—as courts have pointed out—it's direct evidence of sex discrimination. If that's not motivation enough, evaluators can miss critical skills by focusing on personality. It's more valuable, and accurate, to say someone is a strong collaborator who can manage projects across multiple departments than to say "She's friendly and gets along with everyone."

3. Level the playing field with respect to self-promotion

The modesty mandate mentioned above prevents many people in out-groups from writing effective self-evaluations or defending themselves at review time. Counter that by giving everyone you manage the tools to evaluate their own performance. Be clear that it's acceptable, and even expected, to advocate for oneself. A simple two-pager can help overcome the modesty mandate and cue majority men (who tend toward overconfidence) to provide concrete evidence for their claims.

4. Explain how training, promotion, and pay decisions will be made, and follow those rules

As the chair of her firm's women's initiative, one lawyer we know developed a strategy to ensure that all candidates for promotion were considered fairly. She started with a clear outline of what was needed to advance and then assigned every eligible employee (already anonymized) to one of three groups: green (meets the objective metrics), yellow (is close), and red (doesn't). Then she presented the color-coded list to the rest of the evaluation team. By anonymizing the data and pregrouping the candidates by competencies, she ensured that no one was forgotten or recommended owing to in-group favoritism.

All the evaluators were forced to stick to the predetermined benchmarks, and as a result, they tapped the best candidates. (Those in the yellow category were given advice about how to move up to green.) When it comes to promotions, there may be limits to what you can do as an individual manager, but you should push for transparency on the criteria used. When they are explicit, it's harder to bend the rules for in-group members.

Organizational change is crucial, but it doesn't happen overnight. Fortunately, you can begin with all these recommendations *today*.

Originally published in November–December 2019. R1906L

Making the Hybrid Workplace Fair

by Mark Mortensen and Martine Haas

THE EARLY STAGES OF THE COVID-19 pandemic upended much about how we work. What came next was neither the death of the office nor a return to the way things were. Instead, our new reality is hybridity: working with employees who are colocated in the same physical space as well as employees working remotely.

Hybridity promises organizations the benefits of remote working (increased flexibility, reduced carbon footprint, labor-cost optimization, and increased employee satisfaction) alongside the critical strengths of traditional, colocated work (smoother coordination, informal networking, stronger cultural socialization, greater creativity, and face-to-face collaboration). But hybridity is also inextricably tied to power—it creates power differentials within teams that can damage relationships, impede effective collaboration, and ultimately reduce performance. To lead effectively in a hybrid environment, managers must recognize and actively manage the two distinct sources of power that can impede—or facilitate—hybrid work: *hybridity positioning* and *hybridity competence*.

How Hybridity Positioning Affects Power

First, hybridity means that, due to where they're positioned, employees have different access to resources and different levels of visibility—both key sources of power and influence.

Resource access differs depending on whether the employee is located in the office or outside of it. Employees in the office have ready and quick access to technology and infrastructure to support their work. They tend to have faster and easier access to information, and that information tends to be more current and broader (including informal watercooler conversations), which provides them with an edge when it comes to the rapid changes of today's environment. Being in the office also provides access to the emotional and task-based social support provided by peers.

In contrast, employees who work remotely often find their weaker technological setup and infrastructure (slow connections, inability to access certain resources from home, a less sophisticated home-office setup) makes it more difficult to demonstrate their competence. Not being present for informal interactions leaves remote workers feeling out of the loop and last to know. Being remote may also lead employees to feel more isolated and lacking the relationships and connections that provide social support.

Visibility level, or being seen by those in power, is also shaped by an employee's location—especially their location relative to their boss and senior managers. Working in the same space as the boss increases the likelihood that employees' efforts and actions will be recognized and top of mind. Employees who are seen in the hallways are likely to come to mind when it's time to staff an important new project, and their actions on that project are likely to be recognized, resulting in credit for a job well done. Even if the boss is working remotely, when an employee is based in the office, it increases the likelihood that their actions will be seen by others and reported to the boss indirectly. When working remotely, no one sees the late nights or early mornings or how hard employees are working to deliver on their obligations. Credit for a collective output is likely to be unevenly attributed mostly to those who are there in the office and more visible.

Taking these two dimensions of hybridity positioning together, we can understand how hybridity affects each employee in a team or work group by thinking in terms of where the employee and manager are situated.

Idea in Brief

Thanks to the benefits for both employers and employees, hybrid work arrangements are likely here to stay. In order for them to work, though, leaders must understand the power differentials these arrangements create within teams and take steps to level the playing field. Where individuals (including the manager) on a team are located relative to others matters, as do each individual's skills in relationship building. The authors offer four strategies managers can take to address the structurally inevitable differences in power that arise in a hybrid environment. Not doing so can damage relationships, impede effective collaboration, and ultimately reduce performance.

How Hybridity Competence Affects Power

Not all individuals are equally skilled at operating within a hybrid environment. The ability to effectively navigate in a hybrid environment is itself a skill and therefore a source of power. Hybridity requires employees to be ambidextrous—able to balance between and navigate across both worlds—in a way that being fully colocated or fully remote doesn't.

Employees who are strong at relationship building, both face-to-face and virtually, have an advantage in hybrid environments, as do those who are willing to ask for, find, and claim the resources they may not have easy access to. Employees with good network and political awareness are able to recognize advantageous positions and situations, and those who establish strong relationships that can transcend the gap between face-to-face and remote working can use informal connections to replace missing information. Hybrid environments reward employees who think and act adaptably and flexibly, who are able to organize and coordinate across a complex and dynamic environment, and who are able to establish and provide evidence of their own trustworthiness when working in a context of low visibility.

On the other hand, employees who are less effective at building relationships in either in-person or remote environments may find themselves struggling to work with collaborators who do work that way. Those who are less skilled at coordinating work within such a complex system may find they're constantly out of sync with colleagues and managers.

Hybridity competence is a separate source of power from hybridity positioning. Someone in a disadvantaged position may still be able to work very effectively if they have high hybridity competence, while someone in an advantaged position may still be ineffective if they have low hybridity competence.

The Managerial Challenge

While employees need to ensure that they're visible to their managers and can access the resources they need for their work, managers similarly need to make sure they stay informed about what their employees are doing and facilitate their access to those resources.

Managers who are colocated with their employees have more information about what and how those employees are doing. Managers who are remote from their employees may feel like they're operating in the dark. Incomplete information is nothing new, but hybridity's real threat is to fairness. Here are four ways managers can actively handle the structurally inevitable differences in power that arise in a hybrid environment and their effects.

Track and communicate

Create an accurate map of your team's "hybridity configuration": who is working where, and when. Once you've mapped this out, you need to have a conversation with them to surface the challenges they and you face and discuss what you can do to overcome them. Always bear in mind that your employees' resource access depends on their location, and their visibility depends on their location relative to you.

Making this task more complex is that hybridity is itself dynamic—a result of variations both across employees ("Martine works in the office, Mark works from home") and for individual employees ("I work in the office MWF and at home TT"). This makes hybridity a moving target. It requires ongoing systematic tracking, codifying, and visualizing to help both managers and employees stay aware of the configuration of hybridity in a given work group and manage the resulting power dynamics.

Design

While some level of power imbalance is structurally inevitable in a hybrid team or work group, when necessary and possible, managers should intervene to redistribute power through shifting access to resources and/or visibility levels.

At the same time, policies and procedures should be revisited regularly to ensure they don't provide an unfair advantage based on hybridity—for example, KPIs that don't align with resource accessibility, or evaluations that don't account for differences in visibility levels.

Educate

Many of these issues arise not solely from hybridity itself but from a lack of awareness of the power imbalances it creates. To effectively manage in hybrid environments, managers must promote awareness of the issues and educate employees (and themselves) on how to avoid bias.

It is particularly important to establish a culture of psychological safety and trust, both individual and collective. This will increase the likelihood of employees speaking up and asking for resources when they need them, as well as boost their confidence that their efforts will be recognized.

Monitor

With this understanding in mind, it's important that managers keep an eye out for key intervention moments. Through our discussions with executives, we've identified a number of key opportunities to address the potential challenges of hybridity for power dynamics within their teams:

- *Performance reviews and evaluations.* Managers must remain acutely aware of how hybridity creates an imbalance in their teams with respect to employees' access to resources and visibility levels, as well as the information that they hold about their employees. Reviews present an opportunity for managers and employees to examine and discuss imbalances and how to address them going forward.

- *Team launches.* Hybrid teams start with team members who are not on the same footing. Team launches are an opportunity for managers and team members to recognize, acknowledge, and discuss power differences and to collectively decide how to manage them.

- *Onboarding.* How can managers bring people into the organization when not everyone can physically come to the office? How can they put their new remote hires on a comparable footing to those who are brought into a face-to-face office environment? Hybridity's impacts on group dynamics need to be incorporated into onboarding sessions and discussions in order to ensure new employees recognize the importance of consciously managing hybridity-based sources of power.

For companies to reap the many benefits of hybrid working, managers must be aware of the power dynamics at play. It's critical that they develop an understanding of hybridity positioning and hybridity competence and take steps to level the playing field for their teams.

Originally published on hbr.org on February 24, 2021. Reprint H067B7

Why Strategy Execution Unravels—and What to Do About It

by Donald Sull, Rebecca Homkes, and Charles Sull

SINCE MICHAEL PORTER'S seminal work in the 1980s we have had a clear and widely accepted definition of what strategy is—but we know a lot less about translating a strategy into results. Books and articles on strategy outnumber those on execution by an order of magnitude. And what little has been written on execution tends to focus on tactics or generalize from a single case. So what do we know about strategy execution?

We know that it matters. A recent survey of more than 400 global CEOs found that executional excellence was the number one challenge facing corporate leaders in Asia, Europe, and the United States, heading a list of some 80 issues, including innovation, geopolitical instability, and top-line growth. We also know that execution is difficult. Studies have found that two-thirds to three-quarters of large organizations struggle to implement their strategies.

Nine years ago one of us (Don) began a large-scale project to understand how complex organizations can execute their strategies more effectively. The research includes more than 40 experiments in which we made changes in companies and measured the impact on execution, along with a survey administered to nearly 8,000 managers in more than 250 companies (see the sidebar "About the

Research"). The study is ongoing but has already produced valuable insights. The most important one is this: Several widely held beliefs about how to implement strategy are just plain wrong. In this article we debunk five of the most pernicious myths and replace them with a more accurate perspective that will help managers effectively execute strategy.

Myth 1: Execution Equals Alignment

Over the past few years we have asked managers from hundreds of companies, before they take our survey, to describe how strategy is executed in their firms. Their accounts paint a remarkably consistent picture. The steps typically consist of translating strategy into objectives, cascading those objectives down the hierarchy, measuring progress, and rewarding performance. When asked how they would improve execution, the executives cite tools, such as management by objectives and the balanced scorecard, that are designed to increase alignment between activities and strategy up and down the chain of command. In the managers' minds, execution equals alignment, so a failure to execute implies a breakdown in the processes to link strategy to action at every level in the organization.

Despite such perceptions, it turns out that in the vast majority of companies we have studied, those processes are sound. Research on strategic alignment began in the 1950s with Peter Drucker's work on management by objectives, and by now we know a lot about achieving alignment. Our research shows that best practices are well established in today's companies. More than 80% of managers say that their goals are limited in number, specific, and measurable and that they have the funds needed to achieve them. If most companies are doing everything right in terms of alignment, why are they struggling to execute their strategies?

To find out, we ask survey respondents how frequently they can count on others to deliver on promises—a reliable measure of whether things in an organization get done (see "Promise-Based Management: The Essence of Execution," by Donald N. Sull and Charles Spinosa, HBR, April 2007). Fully 84% of managers say they

Idea in Brief

The Problem

We have thousands of guides about developing a strategy—but very few about how to actually execute one. And the difficulty of achieving executional excellence is a major obstacle at most companies.

The Research

Executives attribute poor execution to a lack of alignment and a weak performance culture.

It turns out, though, that in most businesses activities line up well with strategic goals, and the people who meet their numbers are consistently rewarded.

The Recommendations

To execute their strategies, companies must foster coordination across units and build the agility to adapt to changing market conditions.

can rely on their boss and their direct reports all or most of the time—a finding that would make Drucker proud but sheds little light on why execution fails. When we ask about commitments across functions and business units, the answer becomes clear. Only 9% of managers say they can rely on colleagues in other functions and units all the time, and just half say they can rely on them most of the time. Commitments from these colleagues are typically not much more reliable than promises made by external partners, such as distributors and suppliers.

When managers cannot rely on colleagues in other functions and units, they compensate with a host of dysfunctional behaviors that undermine execution: They duplicate effort, let promises to customers slip, delay their deliverables, or pass up attractive opportunities. The failure to coordinate also leads to conflicts between functions and units, and these are handled badly two times out of three—resolved after a significant delay (38% of the time), resolved quickly but poorly (14%), or simply left to fester (12%).

Even though, as we've seen, managers typically equate execution with alignment, they do recognize the importance of coordination when questioned about it directly. When asked to identify the single greatest challenge to executing their company's strategy, 30% cite failure to coordinate across units, making that a close second to failure to align (40%). Managers also say they are three times more

About the Research

FIVE YEARS AGO we developed an in-depth survey that we have administered to 7,600 managers in 262 companies across 30 industries to date. We used the following principles in its design.

Focus on complex organizations in volatile markets. The companies in our sample are typically large (6,000 employees, on average, and median annual sales of $430 million) and compete in volatile sectors: Financial services, information technology, telecommunications, and oil and gas are among the most highly represented. One-third are based in emerging markets.

Target those in the know. We ask companies to identify the leaders most critical to driving execution, and we send the survey to those named. On average, 30 managers per company respond. They represent multiple organizational layers, including top team members (13%), their direct reports (28%), other middle managers (25%), frontline supervisors and team leaders (20%), and technical and domain experts and others (14%).

Gather objective data. Whenever possible, we structure questions to elicit objective information. For example, to assess how well executives communicate strategy, we ask respondents to list their companies' strategic priorities for the next few years; we then code the responses and test their convergence with one another and their consistency with management's stated objectives.

Engage the respondents. To prevent respondents from "checking out," we vary question formats and pose questions that managers view as important and have not been asked before. More than 95% of respondents finish the survey, spending an average of 40 minutes on it.

Link to credible research. Although the research on execution as a whole is not very advanced, some components of execution, such as goal setting, team dynamics, and resource allocation, are well understood. Whenever possible, we draw on research findings to design our questions and interpret our results.

---

likely to miss performance commitments because of insufficient support from other units than because of their own teams' failure to deliver.

Whereas companies have effective processes for cascading goals downward in the organization, their systems for managing horizontal performance commitments lack teeth. More than 80% of the companies we have studied have at least one formal system for managing commitments across silos, including cross-functional committees, service-level agreements, and centralized project-management offices—but only 20% of managers believe that these systems work well all or most of the time. More than half want more structure in the processes to coordinate activities across units—twice the number who want more structure in the management-by-objectives system.

Myth 2: Execution Means Sticking to the Plan

When crafting strategy, many executives create detailed road maps that specify who should do what, by when, and with what resources. The strategic-planning process has received more than its share of criticism, but, along with the budgeting process, it remains the backbone of execution in many organizations. Bain & Company, which regularly surveys large corporations around the world about their use of management tools, finds that strategic planning consistently heads the list. After investing enormous amounts of time and energy formulating a plan and its associated budget, executives view deviations as a lack of discipline that undercuts execution.

Unfortunately, no Gantt chart survives contact with reality. No plan can anticipate every event that might help or hinder a company trying to achieve its strategic objectives. Managers and employees at every level need to adapt to facts on the ground, surmount unexpected obstacles, and take advantage of fleeting opportunities. Strategy execution, as we define the term, consists of seizing opportunities that support the strategy while coordinating with other parts of the organization on an ongoing basis. When managers come up with creative solutions to unforeseen problems or run with unexpected opportunities, they are not undermining systematic implementation; they are demonstrating execution at its best.

Such real-time adjustments require firms to be agile. Yet a lack of agility is a major obstacle to effective execution among the companies we have studied. When asked to name the greatest challenge their companies will face in executing strategy over the next few years, nearly one-third of managers cite difficulties adapting to changing market circumstances. It's not that companies fail to adapt at all: Only one manager in 10 saw that as the problem.

Where Execution Breaks Down

OVER THE PAST FIVE YEARS the authors have surveyed nearly 8,000 managers in more than 250 companies about strategy execution. The responses paint a remarkably consistent picture.

We can rely on people in the chain of command, suggesting that alignment up and down the hierarchy is not a problem.

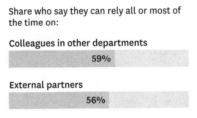

Share of managers who say they can rely all or most of the time on:

Their boss

84%

Their direct reports

84%

But coordination is a problem: People in other units are not much more reliable than external partners are.

Share who say they can rely all or most of the time on:

Colleagues in other departments

59%

External partners

56%

But most organizations either react so slowly that they can't seize fleeting opportunities or mitigate emerging threats (29%), or react quickly but lose sight of company strategy (24%). Just as managers want more structure in the processes to support coordination, they crave more structure in the processes used to adapt to changing circumstances.

A seemingly easy solution would be to do a better job of resource allocation. Although resource allocation is unquestionably critical to execution, the term itself is misleading. In volatile markets, the allotment of funds, people, and managerial attention is not a onetime decision; it requires ongoing adjustment. According to a study by McKinsey, firms that actively *reallocated* capital expenditures across business units achieved an average shareholder return

We don't adapt quickly enough to changing market conditions.

Share who say their organizations effectively:

Shift funds across units to support strategy

30%

Shift people across units to support strategy

20%

Exit declining businesses/unsuccessful initiatives

22%

And we invest in too many nonstrategic projects.

Share who say:

They could secure resources to pursue attractive opportunities outside their strategic objectives

51%

All their company's strategic priorities have the resources they need for success

11%

30% higher than the average return of companies that were slow to shift funds.

Instead of focusing on resource allocation, with its connotation of one-off choices, managers should concentrate on the fluid reallocation of funds, people, and attention. We have noticed a pattern among the companies in our sample: Resources are often trapped in unproductive uses. Fewer than one-third of managers believe that their organizations reallocate funds to the right places quickly enough to be effective. The reallocation of people is even worse. Only 20% of managers say their organizations do a good job of shifting people across units to support strategic priorities. The rest report that their companies rarely shift people across units (47%) or else make shifts in ways that disrupt other units (33%).

Companies also struggle to disinvest. Eight in 10 managers say their companies fail to exit declining businesses or to kill unsuccessful initiatives quickly enough. Failure to exit undermines execution in an obvious way, by wasting resources that could be redeployed. Slow exits impede execution in more-insidious ways as well: Top executives devote a disproportionate amount of time and attention to businesses with limited upside and send in talented managers who often burn themselves out trying to save businesses that should have been shut down or sold years earlier. The longer top executives drag their feet, the more likely they are to lose the confidence of their middle managers, whose ongoing support is critical for execution.

A word of warning: Managers should not invoke agility as an excuse to chase every opportunity that crosses their path. Many companies in our sample lack strategic discipline when deciding which new opportunities to pursue. Half the middle managers we have surveyed believe that they could secure significant resources to pursue attractive opportunities that fall *outside* their strategic objectives. This may sound like good news for any individual manager, but it spells trouble for a company as a whole, leading to the pursuit of more initiatives than resources can support. Only 11% of the managers we have surveyed believe that all their company's strategic priorities have the financial and human resources needed for success. That's a shocking statistic: It means that nine managers in 10 expect some of their organizations' major initiatives to fail for lack of resources. Unless managers screen opportunities against company strategy, they will waste time and effort on peripheral initiatives and deprive the most promising ones of the resources they need to win big. Agility is critical to execution, but it must fit within strategic boundaries. In other words, agility must be balanced with alignment.

Myth 3: Communication Equals Understanding

Many executives believe that relentlessly communicating strategy is a key to success. The CEO of one London-based professional services firm met with her management team the first week of every month and began each meeting by reciting the firm's strategy and its key priorities for the year. She was delighted when an employee engagement survey (not ours) revealed that 84% of all staff members agreed with the statement "I am clear on our organization's top priorities." Her efforts seemed to be paying off.

Then her management team took our survey, which asks members to describe the firm's strategy in their own words and to list the top five strategic priorities. Fewer than one-third could name even two. The CEO was dismayed—after all, she discussed those objectives in every management meeting. Unfortunately, she is not alone. Only 55% of the middle managers we have surveyed can name even one of their company's top five priorities. In other words, when the leaders charged with explaining strategy to the troops are given five chances to list their company's strategic objectives, nearly half fail to get even one right.

Not only are strategic objectives poorly understood, but they often seem unrelated to one another and disconnected from the overall strategy. Just over half of all top team members say they have a clear sense of how major priorities and initiatives fit together. It's pretty dire when half the C-suite cannot connect the dots between strategic priorities, but matters are even worse elsewhere. Fewer than one-third of senior executives' direct reports clearly understand the connections between corporate priorities, and the share plummets to 16% for frontline supervisors and team leaders.

Senior executives are often shocked to see how poorly their company's strategy is understood throughout the organization. In their view, they invest huge amounts of time communicating strategy, in an unending stream of e-mails, management meetings, and town hall discussions. But the amount of communication is not the issue: Nearly 90% of middle managers believe that top leaders communicate the strategy frequently enough. How can so much communication yield so little understanding?

Part of the problem is that executives measure communication in terms of inputs (the number of e-mails sent or town halls hosted) rather than by the only metric that actually counts—how well key leaders understand what's communicated. A related problem occurs when executives dilute their core messages with peripheral considerations. The executives at one tech company, for example, went to great pains to present their company's strategy and objectives at the annual executive off-site. But they also introduced 11 corporate priorities (which were different from the strategic objectives), a list of core competencies (including one with nine templates), a set of corporate values, and a dictionary of 21 new strategic terms to be mastered. Not surprisingly, the assembled managers were baffled about what mattered most. When asked about obstacles to understanding the strategy, middle managers are four times more likely to cite a large number of corporate priorities and strategic initiatives than to mention a lack of clarity in communication. Top executives add to the confusion when they change their messages frequently—a problem flagged by nearly one-quarter of middle managers.

Myth 4: A Performance Culture Drives Execution

When their companies fail to translate strategy into results, many executives point to a weak performance culture as the root cause. The data tells a different story. It's true that in most companies, the official culture—the core values posted on the company website, say—does not support execution. However, a company's true values reveal themselves when managers make hard choices—and here we have found that a focus on performance *does* shape behavior on a day-to-day basis.

Few choices are tougher than personnel decisions. When we ask about factors that influence who gets hired, praised, promoted, and fired, we see that most companies do a good job of recognizing and rewarding performance. Past performance is by far the most frequently named factor in promotion decisions, cited by two-thirds of all managers. Although harder to assess when bringing in new employees, it ranks among the top three influences on who gets hired. One-third of managers believe that performance is also recognized all or most of the time with nonfinancial rewards, such as private praise, public acknowledgment, and access to training opportunities. To be sure, there is room for improvement, particularly when it comes to dealing with underperformers: A majority of the companies we have studied delay action (33%), address underperformance inconsistently (34%), or tolerate poor performance (11%). Overall, though, the companies in our sample have robust performance cultures—and yet they struggle to execute strategy. Why?

The answer is that a culture that supports execution must recognize and reward other things as well, such as agility, teamwork, and ambition. Many companies fall short in this respect. When making hiring or promotion decisions, for example, they place much less value on a manager's ability to adapt to changing circumstances—an indication of the agility needed to execute strategy—than on whether she has hit her numbers in the past. Agility requires a willingness to experiment, and many managers avoid experimentation because they fear the consequences of failure. Half the managers we have surveyed believe that their careers would suffer if they pursued but failed at novel opportunities or innovations. Trying new things inevitably entails setbacks, and honestly discussing the challenges involved increases the odds of long-term success. But corporate cultures rarely support the candid discussions necessary for agility. Fewer than one-third of managers say they can have open and honest discussions about the most difficult issues, while one-third say that many important issues are considered taboo.

An excessive emphasis on performance can impair execution in another subtle but important way. If managers believe that hitting their numbers trumps all else, they tend to make conservative performance commitments. When asked what advice they would give to a new colleague, two-thirds say they would recommend making commitments that the colleague could be sure to meet; fewer than one-third would recommend stretching for ambitious goals. This tendency to play it safe may lead managers to favor surefire cost reductions over risky growth, for instance, or to milk an existing business rather than experiment with a new business model.

The most pressing problem with many corporate cultures, however, is that they fail to foster the coordination that, as we've discussed, is essential to execution. Companies consistently get this wrong. When it comes to hires, promotions, and nonfinancial recognition, past performance is two or three times more likely than a track record of collaboration to be rewarded. Performance is critical, of course, but if it comes at the expense of coordination, it can undermine execution. We ask respondents what would happen to a manager in their organization who achieved his objectives but failed to collaborate with colleagues in other units. Only 20% believe the behavior would be addressed promptly; 60% believe it would be addressed inconsistently or after a delay; and 20% believe it would be tolerated.

Myth 5: Execution Should Be Driven from the Top

In his best-selling book *Execution,* Larry Bossidy describes how, as the CEO of AlliedSignal, he personally negotiated performance objectives with managers several levels below him and monitored their progress. Accounts like this reinforce the common image of a heroic CEO perched atop the org chart, driving execution. That approach can work—for a while. AlliedSignal's stock outperformed the market under Bossidy's leadership. However, as Bossidy writes, shortly after he retired "the discipline of execution...unraveled," and the company gave up its gains relative to the S&P 500.

Top-down execution has drawbacks in addition to the risk of unraveling after the departure of a strong CEO. To understand why, it helps to remember that effective execution in large, complex organizations emerges from countless decisions and actions at all levels. Many of those involve hard trade-offs: For example, synching up with colleagues in another unit can slow down a team that's trying to seize a fleeting opportunity, and screening customer requests against strategy often means turning away lucrative business. The leaders who are closest to the situation and can respond most quickly are best positioned to make the tough calls.

Concentrating power at the top may boost performance in the short term, but it degrades an organization's capacity to execute over the long run. Frequent and direct intervention from on high encourages middle managers to escalate conflicts rather than resolve them, and over time they lose the ability to work things out with colleagues in other units. Moreover, if top executives insist on making the important calls themselves, they diminish middle managers' decision-making skills, initiative, and ownership of results.

In large, complex organizations, execution lives and dies with a group we call "distributed leaders," which includes not only middle managers who run critical businesses and functions but also technical and domain experts who occupy key spots in the informal networks that get things done. The vast majority of these leaders try to do the right thing. Eight out of 10 in our sample say they are committed to doing their best to execute the strategy, even when they would like more clarity on what the strategy is.

Distributed leaders, not senior executives, represent "management" to most employees, partners, and customers. Their day-to-day actions, particularly how they handle difficult decisions and what behaviors they tolerate, go a long way toward supporting or undermining the corporate culture. In this regard, most distributed leaders shine. As assessed by their direct reports, more than 90% of middle managers live up to the organization's values all or most of the time. They do an especially good job of reinforcing performance, with nearly nine in 10 consistently holding team members accountable for results.

But although execution should be driven from the middle, it needs to be guided from the top. And our data suggests that many top executive teams could provide much more support. Distributed leaders are hamstrung in their efforts to translate overall company strategy into terms meaningful for their teams or units when top executives fail to ensure that they clearly understand that strategy. And as we've seen, such failure is not the exception but the rule.

Conflicts inevitably arise in any organization where different units pursue their own objectives. Distributed leaders are asked to shoulder much of the burden of working across silos, and many appear to be buckling under the load. A minority of middle managers consistently anticipate and avoid problems (15%) or resolve conflicts quickly and well (26%). Most resolve issues only after a significant delay (37%), try but fail to resolve them (10%), or don't address them at all (12%). Top executives could help by adding structured processes

SULL, HOMKES, AND SULL

to facilitate coordination. In many cases they could also do a better job of modeling teamwork. One-third of distributed leaders believe that factions exist within the C-suite and that executives there focus on their own agendas rather than on what is best for the company.

Many executives try to solve the problem of execution by reducing it to a single dimension. They focus on tightening alignment up and down the chain of command—by improving existing processes, such as strategic planning and performance management, or adopting new tools, such as the balanced scorecard. These are useful measures, to be sure, but relying on them as the sole means of driving execution ignores the need for coordination and agility in volatile markets. If managers focus too narrowly on improving alignment, they risk developing ever more refined answers to the wrong question.

In the worst cases, companies slip into a dynamic we call the alignment trap. When execution stalls, managers respond by tightening the screws on alignment—tracking more performance metrics, for example, or demanding more-frequent meetings to monitor progress and recommend what to do. This kind of top-down scrutiny often deteriorates into micromanagement, which stifles the experimentation required for agility and the peer-to-peer interactions that drive coordination. Seeing execution suffer but not knowing why, managers turn once more to the tool they know best and further tighten alignment. The end result: Companies are trapped in a downward spiral in which more alignment leads to worse results.

If common beliefs about execution are incomplete at best and dangerous at worst, what should take their place? The starting point is a fundamental redefinition of execution as the ability to seize opportunities aligned with strategy while coordinating with other parts of the organization on an ongoing basis. Reframing execution in those terms can help managers pinpoint why it is stalling. Armed with a more comprehensive understanding, they can avoid pitfalls such as the alignment trap and focus on the factors that matter most for translating strategy into results.

Originally published in March 2015. Reprint R1503C

The Leader as Coach

by Herminia Ibarra and Anne Scoular

ONCE UPON A TIME, MOST PEOPLE began successful careers by developing expertise in a technical, functional, or professional domain. Doing your job well meant having the right answers. If you could prove yourself that way, you'd rise up the ladder and eventually move into people management—at which point you had to ensure that your subordinates had those same answers.

As a manager, you knew what needed to be done, you taught others how to do it, and you evaluated their performance. Command and control was the name of the game, and your goal was to direct and develop employees who understood how the business worked and were able to reproduce its previous successes.

Not today. Rapid, constant, and disruptive change is now the norm, and what succeeded in the past is no longer a guide to what will succeed in the future. Twenty-first-century managers simply don't (and can't!) have all the right answers. To cope with this new reality, companies are moving away from traditional command-and-control practices and toward something very different: a model in which managers give support and guidance rather than instructions, and employees learn how to adapt to constantly changing environments in ways that unleash fresh energy, innovation, and commitment.

The role of the manager, in short, is becoming that of a coach.

This is a dramatic and fundamental shift, and we've observed it firsthand. Over the past decade, we've seen it in our ongoing research on how organizations are transforming themselves for the digital age; we've discerned it from what our executive students and coaching clients have told us about the leadership skills they want to cultivate in themselves and throughout their firms; and we've noticed that more and more of the companies we work with are investing in training their leaders as coaches. Increasingly, coaching is becoming integral to the fabric of a learning culture—a skill that good managers at all levels need to develop and deploy.

We should note that when we talk about coaching, we mean something broader than just the efforts of consultants who are hired to help executives build their personal and professional skills. That work is important and sometimes vital, but it's temporary and executed by outsiders. The coaching we're talking about—the kind that creates a true learning organization—is ongoing and executed by those inside the organization. It's work that all managers should engage in with all their people all the time, in ways that help define the organization's culture and advance its mission. An effective manager-as-coach asks questions instead of providing answers, supports employees instead of judging them, and facilitates their development instead of dictating what has to be done.

This conception of coaching represents an evolution. Coaching is no longer just a benevolent form of sharing what you know with somebody less experienced or less senior, although that remains a valuable aspect. It's also a way of asking questions so as to spark insights in the other person. As Sir John Whitmore, a leading figure in the field, defined it, skilled coaching involves "unlocking people's potential to maximize their own performance." The best practitioners have mastered both parts of the process—imparting knowledge and helping others discover it themselves—and they can artfully do both in different situations.

It's one thing to aspire to that kind of coaching, but it's another to make it happen as an everyday practice throughout the many layers of an organization. At most firms, a big gap still yawns between aspiration and practice—and we've written this article to help readers bridge it. We focus first on how to develop coaching as an individual managerial capacity, and then on how to make it an organizational one.

Idea in Brief

The Situation

To cope with disruptive change, companies are reinventing themselves as learning organizations. This requires a new approach to management in which leaders serve as coaches to those they supervise.

The Challenge

In this new approach, managers ask questions instead of providing answers, support employees instead of judging them, and facilitate their development instead of dictating what has to be done. But most managers don't feel they have time for that—and they're not very good at it anyway.

The Solution

Companies need to offer their managers the appropriate tools and support to become better coaches. And if they want to be sustainably healthy learning organizations, they must also develop coaching as an organizational capacity.

You're Not as Good as You Think

For leaders who are accustomed to tackling performance problems by telling people what to do, a coaching approach often feels too "soft." What's more, it can make them psychologically uncomfortable, because it deprives them of their most familiar management tool: asserting their authority. So they resist coaching—and left to their own devices, they may not even give it a try. "I'm too busy," they'll say, or "This isn't the best use of my time," or "The people I'm saddled with aren't coachable." In Daniel Goleman's classic study of leadership styles, published in HBR in 2000, leaders ranked coaching as their least-favorite style, saying they simply didn't have time for the slow and tedious work of teaching people and helping them grow.

Even if many managers are unenthusiastic about coaching, most think they're pretty good at it. But a lot of them are not. In one study, 3,761 executives assessed their own coaching skills, and then their assessments were compared with those of people who worked with them. The results didn't align well. Twenty-four percent of the executives significantly overestimated their abilities, rating themselves as above average while their colleagues ranked them in the bottom third of the group. That's a telling mismatch. "If you think you're a good coach but you actually aren't," the authors of the study wrote, "this data suggests you may be a good deal worse than you imagined."

Coaching well can be hard for even the most competent and well-meaning of managers. One of us (Herminia) teaches a class to executives that makes this clear year after year. The executives are given a case study and asked to play the role of a manager who must decide whether to fire or coach a direct report who is not performing up to par. The employee has made obvious errors of judgment, but the manager has contributed significantly to the problem by having alternately ignored and micromanaged him.

When presented with this scenario, nine out of 10 executives decide they want to help their direct report do better. But when they're asked to role-play a coaching conversation with him, they demonstrate much room for improvement. They know what they're supposed to do: "ask and listen," not "tell and sell." But that doesn't come naturally, because deep down they've already made up their minds about the right way forward, usually before they even begin talking to the employee. So their efforts to coach typically consist of just trying to get agreement on what they've already decided. That's not real coaching—and not surprisingly, it doesn't play out well.

Here's roughly how these conversations unfold. The executives begin with an open-ended question, such as "How do you think things are going?" This invariably elicits an answer very different from what they expected. So they reformulate the question, but this, too, fails to evoke the desired response. With some frustration, they start asking leading questions, such as "Don't you think your personal style would be a better fit in a different role?" This makes the direct report defensive, and he becomes even less likely to give the hoped-for answer. Eventually, feeling that the conversation is going nowhere, the executives switch into "tell" mode to get their conclusion across. At the end of the exercise, no one has learned anything about the situation or themselves.

Sound familiar? This kind of "coaching" is all too common, and it holds companies back in their attempts to become learning organizations. The good news, though, is that with the right tools and support, a sound method, and lots of practice and feedback, almost anybody can become a better coach.

Different Ways of Helping

To get managers thinking about the nature of coaching, and specifically how to do it better in the context of a learning organization, we like to present them with the 2x2 matrix in the exhibit "Styles of coaching." It's a simple but useful tool. One axis shows the information, advice, or expertise that a coach *puts in* to the relationship with the person being coached; the other shows the motivational energy that a coach *pulls out* by unlocking that person's own insights and solutions.

At the upper left, in quadrant 1, is *directive coaching,* which takes place primarily through "telling." Mentoring falls into this category. Everybody knows what to expect here: A manager with years of accumulated knowledge willingly shares it with a junior team member, and that person listens carefully, hoping to absorb as much knowledge as possible. This approach has a lot to recommend it, but it has some downsides too. Because it consists of stating what to do and how to do it, it unleashes little energy in the person being

Styles of coaching

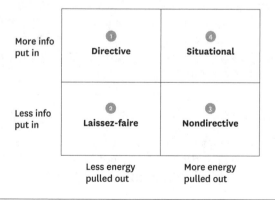

coached; indeed, it may even depress her energy level and motivation. It also assumes that the boss knows things that the recipient of the coaching does not—not always a safe assumption in a complex and constantly changing work environment. Additionally, because it allows leaders to continue doing what they have always excelled at (solving other people's problems), it does not build organizational capacity well.

That said, coaching is not always the answer. There may be times when all team members are productively getting on with their work, and the right approach to managing them is to leave them alone. This approach, which we call *laissez-faire*, appears in quadrant 2.

At the bottom right, in quadrant 3, is *nondirective coaching*, which is built on listening, questioning, and withholding judgment. Managers here work to draw wisdom, insight, and creativity out of the people they're coaching, with the goal of helping them learn to resolve problems and cope with challenging situations on their own. It's an approach that can be highly energizing for those being coached, but it doesn't come naturally to most managers, who tend to be more comfortable in "tell" mode.

At the top right, in quadrant 4, is *situational coaching*, which represents the sweet spot in our framework. All managers in a learning organization should aspire to become expert at situational coaching—which, as its name suggests, involves striking a fine balance between directive and nondirective styles according to the specific needs of the moment. From our work with experienced executives, we've concluded that managers should first practice nondirective coaching a lot on its own, until it becomes almost second nature, and only then start to balance that newly strengthened ability with periods of helpful directive coaching.

The GROW Model

One of the best ways to get better at nondirective coaching is to try conversing using the GROW model, devised in the 1980s by Sir John Whitmore and others. GROW involves four action steps, the first letters of which give the model its name. It's easy to grasp conceptually, but it's harder to practice than you might imagine, because it requires training yourself to think in new ways about what your role and value are as a leader. The four action steps are these:

Goal

When you begin discussing a topic with someone you're coaching, establish exactly what he wants to accomplish *right now*. Not what his goals are for the project or his job or his role in the organization, but what he hopes to get out of this particular exchange. People don't do this organically in most conversations, and they often need help with it. A good way to start is to ask something like "What do you want when you walk out the door that you don't have now?"

Reality

With the goal of your conversation established, ask questions rooted in *what, when, where,* and *who,* each of which forces people to come down out of the clouds and focus on specific facts. This makes the conversation real and constructive. You'll notice that we didn't include *why.* That's because asking why demands that people explore reasons and motivations rather than facts. In doing that, it can carry overtones of judgment or trigger attempts at self-justification, both of which can be counterproductive.

During this stage, a good reality-focused question to ask is "What are the key things we need to know?" Attend carefully to how people respond. Are they missing something important? Are they talking about operational issues but forgetting the human side of the equation? Or the reverse? When you ask people to slow down and think in this way, they often lose themselves in contemplation—and then a light comes on, and off they go, engaging with the problem on their own with new energy and a fresh perspective. This step is critical, because it stops people from overlooking pertinent variables and leaping to conclusions. Your job here is just to raise the right questions and then get out of the way.

Coaching 101

START with a few basic steps.

Assess the Situation

Decide what kind of coaching is necessary. Full situational coaching—balancing directive and nondirective coaching moment by moment—isn't always the answer. There will always be scenarios in which people simply need to be told what to do. At other times—if, say, they're struggling with deeply important career decisions—it might be appropriate to offer nondirective coaching but nothing more. It's also possible that your people don't need any coaching right now but would really value an ear later. Ask them.

Listen

Here's a good rule of thumb for most situations: Shut up and listen. Absorb what people tell you, and be alert to what their tone of voice and body language convey. Don't respond as you usually might; instead, listen just to understand. Occasionally repeat back what you hear, to make sure you have it right, but avoid jumping in. Leave room for silence, especially at the end of your conversation. The most important things often emerge from that silence.

Options

When people come to you for coaching, they often feel stuck. "There's nothing I can do," they might tell you. Or "I have only one real option." Or "I'm torn between A and B."

At this point your task is to help them think more broadly and more deeply. To broaden the conversation, sometimes it's enough to ask something as simple as "If you had a magic wand, what would you do?" You'd be surprised how freeing many people find that question to be—and how quickly they then start thinking in fresh, productive ways. Once they've broadened their perspective and discovered new options, your job is to prompt them to deepen their thinking, perhaps by encouraging them to explore the upside, the downside, and the risks of each option.

Will

This step also doesn't usually happen organically in conversations, so again most people will need help with it. The step actually has two parts, each involving a different sense of the word *will*.

Ask Open-Ended Questions

Yes/no questions shut down thinking. Open-ended ones expand it. The coaching thought leader Nancy Kline uses a provocative one that goes roughly like this: "What do you already know, without being aware of it, that you will find out in a year?" But the questions don't have to be complex or clever. Sometimes the simplest—such as "What else?"—are the best. What's vital is that they demonstrate your authentic interest and belief in the person you are coaching. That's something to work hard on, even if the person's performance to date has you doubtful. If you can sincerely suspend judgment, you may be surprised!

Practice Nondirective Coaching

Practice makes perfect. Try nondirective coaching outside of work—perhaps in some pro bono or other extracurricular role. Practice it in a disciplined, sustained way until you have confidence you're doing it well. You'll know you're getting good when the people you're talking with start to have "Aha!" moments or thank you profusely even though you feel you didn't tell them anything.

In the first part you ask, "What will you do?" This encourages the person you're coaching to review the specific action plan that has emerged from your conversation. If the conversation has gone well, she'll have a clear sense of what that plan is. If she doesn't, you'll need to cycle back through the earlier steps of the GROW process and help her define how she'll attack the problem.

The second part involves asking people about their will to act. "On a scale of one to 10," you might ask, "how likely is it that you will do this?" If they respond with an eight or higher, they're probably motivated enough to follow through. If the answer is seven or less, they probably won't. In that case you'll again need to cycle back through the earlier steps of the process, in an effort to arrive at a solution they are more likely to act on.

Of course, workplace coaching usually takes place outside of formal coaching sessions. Most often, it happens in brief exchanges, when a manager might respond to a request for help by posing a single question, such as "What have you already thought of?" or "What really matters here?" When more of those interactions occur—when you notice your managers growing increasingly inquisitive, asking good questions, and working from the premise that they don't have all the answers—you'll know you're on the right track.

Coaching as an Organizational Capacity

So far, we've focused on coaching as a managerial skill. That's a vital first step, but to transform your company into a genuine learning organization, you need to do more than teach individual leaders and managers how to coach better. You also need to make coaching an organizational capacity that fits integrally within your company culture. And to succeed at that, you must effect a cultural transformation that involves the following steps.

Articulate the "why"

Managers and professionals are busy people. If coaching strikes them as simply the latest fad being pushed by HR, they will roll their eyes and comply with the requirements as minimally as possible. If you want them to embrace coaching as not just a personal skill but also a source of cultural strength, you'll have to make clear why it's valuable for the business and their own success.

A good "why" inevitably connects coaching to an organization's mission-critical tasks. Consider the example of the international law firm Allen & Overy. When David Morley, then the senior partner, decided to make coaching a key part of the firm's leadership culture, he began talking with his colleagues about the importance of high-value conversations. Morley is an alumnus of one of our (Anne's) leadership coach trainings. "My pitch," he told us, "was this: 'As a senior leader, you have roughly 100 conversations a year that are of particularly high value—in the sense that they will change your life or the life of the person you're talking to. We want to help you acquire the skills to maximize value in those 100 conversations, to unlock previously hidden issues, to uncover new options, and to reveal fresh insights.' That resonated. Almost everybody in a key leadership position at the firm recognized that they struggled with how to make the most of those conversations, and they could readily see that they lacked skills."

Articulating the "why" can also involve helping people see the collateral benefits of coaching. That's what worked at the Berkeley Partnership, an international management consultancy, where many partners who have received our training in coaching tell us it has significantly enhanced their ability to serve their clients. According to Mark Fearn, one of the firm's founders, Berkeley partners are now better equipped to respond when clients ask for assistance with big, messy, sometimes ill-defined problems that often extend far beyond the firm's initial brief. Having developed their coaching skills, partners have become better at recognizing situations in which they don't have to provide answers; they understand that in such cases, they may be able to offer more value by listening attentively, asking the right questions, and supporting clients as they work out the best solution. "Now that we've added coaching expertise," Fearn told us, "our task can sometimes be just digging the answer out of them, creating a space to think."

Model the behavior
If you want the people you work with to embrace coaching, you first need to embrace it yourself.

Nobody has done this better than Satya Nadella, the CEO of Microsoft. As noted in a London Business School case study that Herminia cowrote, when Nadella took the reins, in 2014, he was only the third chief executive in the company's four-decade history. During the 14-year tenure of his predecessor, Steve Ballmer, revenue had tripled and profits had doubled, but by the end of that time, the company had lost its momentum. A culture of inspection and judgment prevailed, and the managerial mindset was fixed: Managers evaluated direct reports according to how well they mastered skills and generated numbers that would allow them to reproduce the successes of the past.

This culture had contributed significantly to Microsoft's remarkable run of dominance in the world of personal computing. But as the energy in the tech sector shifted to smartphones and the cloud, the old management practices began to impede progress. By the time Nadella took over, risk aversion and internal politics were hampering

Further Reading

Coaching Advice

- "Coaching for Change," Richard Boyatzis, Melvin Smith, and Ellen Van Oosten, HBR, September–October 2019
- "Every Manager Needs to Practice Two Types of Coaching," Dick Grote, HBR.org, September 30, 2016
- "4 Reasons Managers Should Spend More Time on Coaching," Joseph R. Weintraub and James M. Hunt, HBR.org, May 29, 2015
- "Overcoming the Toughest Common Coaching Challenges," Amy Gallo, HBR.org, April 15, 2015

cross-divisional collaboration, senior leaders were resisting open-source innovation, and the company's stock price had stalled. Additionally, technologies were changing so quickly that managers often had out-of-date knowledge and practices, but they kept passing these down because that's what they knew how to do.

Nadella quickly realized that Microsoft needed a cultural transformation. To regain its momentum and assert itself as a force in this new landscape, the company had to move away from its entrenched managerial style and instead develop what the Stanford psychologist Carol Dweck has called a growth mindset, in which everybody in the organization was open to constant learning and risk-taking. As Nadella himself aptly put it, the leaders of the company had to shift from being know-it-alls to being "learn-it-alls."

Nadella understood that the process had to start with him, so he began modeling the behaviors he wanted Microsoft's managers to adopt. He solicited thoughts from everybody he talked to and listened empathetically to what they had to say. He asked nondirective questions, demonstrating that his role was to support rather than judge. He encouraged people to be open about their mistakes and to learn from them. "He's with you," said Jean-Phillipe Courtois, a member of his leadership team. "You can feel it. You can see the body language. It doesn't matter if you're a top executive or a first-line seller; he has exactly the same quality of listening."

Coaching Theory

- *Coaching for Performance: The Principles and Practice of Coaching and Leadership*, Sir John Whitmore and Performance Consultants International, Nicholas Brealey, 2017 (fully revised 25th-anniversary edition)
- *Time to Think: Listening to Ignite the Human Mind*, Nancy Kline, Cassell Illustrated, 1999
- *Humble Inquiry: The Gentle Art of Asking Instead of Telling*, Edgar H. Schein, Berrett-Koehler, 2013

Modeling is powerful because it shows that a leader walks the talk. Moreover, it builds momentum. Researchers have found that when people are in doubt about what behavior is appropriate, they copy the actions of others—particularly those who have power and status. So it's not surprising that in these times of rapid change, which inevitably bring business uncertainty, employees look to their leaders for cues to follow. If they notice that their leaders are working to foster learning and cultivate the delicate art of leadership as conversation, they will do likewise.

Build capability throughout the organization

After Nadella became Microsoft's CEO, the corporate climate changed and the company's performance surged. But Nadella was not single-handedly responsible. With more than 130,000 employees, he depended on the members of his leadership team to tailor the growth mindset to the unique requirements of their individual businesses. For Courtois—who in 2016 assumed control of Microsoft's global sales, marketing, and operations—that meant transforming the culture from one of command and control to one of coaching.

Herminia has studied Microsoft's revival in depth, so we have a clear understanding of how things unfolded. Courtois recognized that the "why" of the shift to coaching was Microsoft's move to a cloud-first strategy. The fundamental economics of cloud computing are based on the premise that customers will pay only for the resources they use (how long a server is utilized, say, or how much data bandwidth is being consumed). With revenue growth now depending more heavily on consumption of Microsoft's offerings, everyone at the company had to become adept at having conversations in which they could learn what they did not already know—how to serve the unmet needs of their customers. And with the availability of powerful digital tools that provided everyone with real-time data on key metrics, it no longer made sense for managers to spend their time monitoring and controlling employees. So, after a restructuring effort aimed at giving Microsoft's sales teams the right technical and industry skills to accompany corporate customers as they moved to the cloud, Courtois followed up with workshops, tools, and an online course designed to help the company's managers develop a coaching style of leadership.

"If we want to get the transformation all the way through the organization," he told us, "our biggest challenge is to reboot our people managers. 'People manager' is a job. You're not just a sales manager, where you have a quota, a territory, customers, partners, and goals to achieve. You're actually someone whose mission it is to pick, grow, and motivate the best capabilities to build customer success."

Remove the barriers
As in many organizations, managerial life at Microsoft had a rhythm dictated by quarterly business reviews. One of those, an annual gathering known as the January midyear review, was one of the most visible manifestations of the command-and-control culture.

Over time, the midyear review had developed into a kind of corporate theater in which the C-suite team, adopting an interrogatory stance, would grill senior managers from around the world on their progress and plans. This format of "precision questioning" ended up having "a fear impact on people," said one executive, "because they felt like they were going into that meeting to be judged personally. So they felt they had to paint the best picture they could without showing any mistakes or failures." Stories abounded of senior managers anxiously beginning their preparation well before the December holiday period. In other words, to make a good impression, a raft of the company's most valuable people were diverting more than a month of their time to preparing for an internal review. As part of the shift to a learning culture, Courtois had already encouraged his team to abandon precision questioning in favor of a more coaching-oriented approach that involved asking questions such as "What are you trying to do?" "What's working?" "What's not working?" and "How can we help?" But old habits die hard. Only after Courtois eliminated the midyear review—thereby removing a significant barrier to change—did everybody understand that he meant business.

Something similar happened at Allen & Overy, where year-end appraisals and rankings had become a largely unproductive ritual. In its push to become a learning organization, the firm recognized that these exercises were a deterrent to the kinds of open and supportive conversations that employees needed both to develop professionally and to advance the organization's mission. It therefore abandoned that performance review system and now trains its partners to engage year-round in coaching conversations with associates, providing them with real-time feedback on their work. Employees report that these conversations create a new and useful level of dialogue about their career development. And once again, there are collateral benefits. Although the program was designed for internal use, it has made the organization's senior leaders more comfortable in conducting unstructured conversations in other contexts, especially during high-stakes client negotiations—and that, in turn, has led to higher revenue and deeper client relationships.

We live in a world of flux. Successful executives must increasingly supplement their industry and functional expertise with a general capacity for learning—and they must develop that capacity in the people they supervise. No longer can managers simply command

and control. Nor will they succeed by rewarding team members mainly for executing flawlessly on things they already know how to do. Instead, with full institutional support, they need to reinvent themselves as coaches whose job it is to draw energy, creativity, and learning out of the people with whom they work.

Originally published in November–December 2019. Reprint R1906G

Make the Most of Your One-on-One Meetings

by Steven G. Rogelberg

TURNOVER WAS HIGH on Bill's team—higher, in fact, than on most other teams at his company. Although Bill thought of himself as a good manager, exit interviews with his departing team members suggested that they hadn't felt meaningfully engaged or fully supported in their roles and had tended to step on one another's toes with their assignments.

What, exactly, was Bill doing wrong? One area stood out when I spoke with him and his team: He held fewer regular one-on-one (1:1) meetings with his direct reports than his peers at the company did. When he did meet with team members individually, the subject tended to be a critical issue he needed help with rather than their work or their development.

Bill, a composite of managers I've worked with and studied, clearly had a blind spot when it came to 1:1s. Such blind spots are not uncommon. Of 250 direct reports I surveyed recently, nearly half rated their 1:1 experiences as suboptimal. That's hardly surprising, given that few organizations provide strong guidance or training for managers about when and how to meet individually with their employees. But my research shows that managers who don't invest in such conversations—who view them as a burden, hold them too infrequently, or manage them poorly—risk leaving their team members disconnected, both functionally and emotionally.

The best managers recognize that 1:1s are not an add-on to their role—they are foundational to it. Those who fully embrace these meetings as the place where leadership happens can make their teams' day-to-day output better and more efficient, build trust and psychological safety, and improve employees' experiences, motivation, and engagement. The managers thrive in turn, because their success is tied to the performance of those reporting to them.

I've been studying teams, leadership, engagement, and meetings at work for decades, and in the past three years I've set out specifically to learn what makes 1:1s work best by doing three studies: a global survey of 1,000 knowledge workers, a U.S. survey of 250 people who either lead or participate in 1:1s, and interviews with nearly 50 top leaders at various *Fortune* 100 companies. I've discovered that although no one-size-fits-all approach exists, there are some useful guidelines for managers. Most important is that the manager should consider the meeting a focused space for the direct report and make that explicit. The meeting should be dominated by topics relating to the needs, concerns, and hopes of the employee, who should take an active role in presenting them. As the manager, your responsibilities are to ensure that the meetings occur, actively facilitate them, encourage genuine conversation, ask good questions, offer support, and help each team member get what's needed for optimal short-term performance and long-term growth.

In this article I'll lay out how to prepare for and facilitate effective 1:1s.

Before the Meetings

Setting up your 1:1s should entail more than dropping invites onto your team members' calendars. You should lay the groundwork for your conversations and plan the logistics to best fit each report's unique needs.

Communicate the initiative or your reboot of the initiative
Whether or not the practice of holding 1:1s is new to your team, announce it at a team meeting so that everyone gets the message at

Idea in Brief

Few organizations provide strong guidance or training for managers on meeting individually with their employees, but the author's research shows that managers who don't hold these meetings frequently enough or who manage them poorly risk leaving their team members disconnected, both functionally and emotionally. When the meetings are done well, they can make a team's day-to-day activities more efficient and better, build trust and psychological safety, and improve employees' experience, motivation, and engagement at work. The author has found that although there's no one-size-fits-all approach to one-on-ones, they are most successful when the meeting is dominated by topics of importance to the direct report rather than issues that are top of mind for the manager. Managers should focus on making sure the meetings take place, creating space for genuine conversation, asking good questions, offering support, and helping team members get what they need to thrive in both their short-term performance and their long-term growth.

the same time and no one feels singled out. Tie the meetings to your organization's values (such as the importance of hearing employees' voices) and to your personal values (such as striving to be a supportive leader). Also stress that these conversations are not meant to signal dissatisfaction with your team's work and are not about micromanaging; rather, they are opportunities for you and each member to get to know each other better, learn about challenges, and discuss careers, and for you to give help when it's needed. This is also a good moment to tell your team members what you need from them to make the meetings successful: They should drive the agenda with key priorities, be curious, be actively engaged, communicate candidly, think deeply about problems and solutions, and be willing to ask for help and act on feedback.

Determine cadence

My research suggests that you should adopt one of three plans for the frequency of 1:1s:

1. You meet with each of your team members *once a week* for 30 minutes or so. In my surveys, employees, regardless of job

level, rated this approach the most desirable; it also correlated with the highest levels of engagement.

2. In the second-highest-rated plan you meet *every other week* for 45 to 60 minutes.

3. In a *hybrid* plan you meet with some team members weekly and others every two weeks.

Whichever plan you choose, aim to spend roughly equivalent amounts of time with employees over the course of a month so that all team members get the same in-person support from you. To determine the right cadence, consider:

- *Team member experience.* Weekly meetings are ideal for more-junior employees and those who are new to the team. They allow you to provide coaching and other support for the employees' growth and development and to build a relationship.

- *Manager tenure.* Similarly, if *you* are new to the team, weekly meetings are ideal for establishing relationships and alignment.

- *Team size.* If your team is large (10 or more), consider holding 1:1s every other week so that you can stagger them across a longer time span. You may need to reduce the time allotted to each meeting. To ease the load associated with a large team, some managers introduce peer mentoring, in which team members give guidance and feedback to one another rather than rely solely on the manager.

- *Remote or in person.* If your team is remote, weekly meetings can help counter a lack of spontaneous face-to-face contact.

- *Team member preference.* Finally, give your employees a voice in the decision.

I've seen some managers, mostly senior leaders, opt for three or four weeks between 1:1s, but investing only 60 minutes or so with each team member every month makes building a trusting relationship difficult. And because more-recent events are easier to recall, the longer time lapse also means that you're less likely to discuss any issues that arose several weeks prior to the meeting. These meetings are most effective when you can build momentum around specific areas of the direct report's activities and growth. A monthly cadence makes that more challenging. But if your team members are seasoned and have worked with you a long time, and you are readily available for impromptu conversations, this cadence can work and is preferable to nothing. However, employees rated this option as least desirable, and it was associated with smaller gains in engagement.

Finally, avoid canceling 1:1s, which can hamper your team members' progress and make them feel that they are low on your priority list. This was one of Bill's problems: He readily canceled these meetings if he got busy. That sometimes demoralized his team members; they also found themselves duplicating efforts or working at cross-purposes because they hadn't had a chance to coordinate their work through Bill. If you must cancel, reschedule the meeting right away, ideally for the same week—even if that means moving the meeting up rather than moving it out. Another option is to reduce the length of the meeting: Some time together is better than none at all.

Set a location

In my research, employees rated virtual 1:1s as slightly less desirable than those held in person, but they rated the ultimate value of the meetings similarly regardless of which form they'd taken. If you can meet in person, choose a location where you and your employee will feel at ease, present, and free of distractions. In my surveys the most highly rated location was the manager's office or a conference room; the lowest was the direct report's office. Support for outside locations, such as coffee shops, or taking a walk near the office, was uneven, so don't assume that everyone would welcome them. Talk to your team members in advance to gauge where they feel most comfortable.

Create an agenda

Many managers assume that 1:1s are too informal to require an agenda, but my research shows that having one is a strong predictor of the effectiveness of the meeting, whether it was created in advance (which is ideal) or at the meeting itself (if necessary).

Even more critical, though, is the employee's involvement in the agenda's creation: Both direct reports and managers rated meetings most highly when the reports contributed to or established the agenda themselves. Bill's habit of organizing his 1:1s around his own priorities and needs meant that his team members' concerns were usually relegated to the end of the meeting—and often went unaddressed if time ran out.

Collaborating on an agenda can be as simple as having each party create a list of topics to discuss. In the meeting the two should work through first the employee's list and then the manager's, as time

---

Sample questions for 1:1s

Work style preferences
- Tell me about the best manager you've ever had. What did that person do that you thought was most effective and helpful?

Well-being and engagement
- What is your favorite part of the job?
- Least favorite?

Roadblocks, obstacles, or concerns
- Is anything slowing you down or blocking you right now?
- How can I help or support you?

Culture and team dynamics
- What aspects of our team culture do you think we should maintain, change, or work on?

Asking for input
- What feedback from me could be helpful—any particular projects, tasks, skills?
- Would you like more or less coaching or direction from me?

Career development and growth
- What would you like to be doing in five years?
- What work are you doing here that is most in line with your long-term goals?

Personal connections
- What are your favorite podcasts, books, or hobbies?

---

allows. (Both should review their notes from previous 1:1s while preparing their lists in case some topic requires follow-up.)

Alternatively, some managers create the agenda from broad questions, such as: What would you like to talk about today? How are things going with you and your team? What are your current priorities, and are there any problems or concerns you would like to talk through? Is there anything I can help you with or anywhere I can better support you? What do I need to know about or understand from your perspective?

A warning: Both these approaches tend to prioritize immediate tactical issues and fires to be put out. However you plan your agendas, periodically weave in longer-horizon topics such as career planning and developmental opportunities—by either taking five or 10 minutes at every meeting to discuss those areas or dedicating one out of every three or four meetings to addressing them. (See the exhibit "Sample questions for 1:1s" to get a sense of issues that should be discussed over time.)

At the Meetings

Once you've prepared for a meeting, a fruitful discussion will depend on your ability to create a setting in which your employee feels comfortable. A valuable 1:1 addresses both the practical needs and the personal needs—to feel respected, heard, valued, trusted, and included—of the employee. To ensure that a meeting does so:

Set the tone

First, be present. Turn off email alerts, put your phone away, and silence text notifications. Remind yourself as the meeting begins that it is fundamentally about your employee's needs, performance, and engagement.

As you go into the meeting, check your emotional state. Research shows that the mood you bring to a meeting has a contagion effect, so start out with energy and optimism. Reiterate your goals and hopes for the meeting and then move to some non-work-related topics, rapport building, wins, or appreciation to generate momentum and foster feelings of psychological safety. One problem for Bill was that he viewed 1:1s as merely another task on his already long list—something to just get done. That affected how he facilitated (or failed to facilitate), how he listened, how he collaborated, and how he engaged.

Listen more than you talk

The biggest predictor of a 1:1's success, according to my research, is the employee's active participation as measured by the amount of time that person talks during the meeting. The ideal is anywhere from 50% to 90%. The agenda will have some influence on that, but you as the manager should carefully avoid talking more than your employee does.

In addition, listen actively to fully understand your direct report before you speak yourself. Display genuine interest without judgment and acknowledge the employee's viewpoint even if you disagree with it. Ask questions that clarify and constructively challenge that viewpoint. Encourage your team member to provide thoughts on the matters at hand and potential solutions to problems. Stay vigilant about your body language and reactions to ensure that you're creating a welcoming and safe space.

Add your perspective

Once you've listened closely, there will be moments in the meeting when you need to contribute your point of view. A 1:1 provides an excellent opportunity for you to give honest and specific feedback on your direct report's perspectives or actions. It is also a good place for you to engage in collaborative problem solving by truly understanding whatever issue is at hand, pooling information, identifying root causes, and creating a solution that both parties feel good about. If the team member's solution is viable—even if it's not better than your own—it's important that you go with it. That sends a strong message and creates more commitment to the team member's proposed path forward.

Be flexible

As you work through your established agenda, allow the conversation to move organically as needed to provide value. Focus on the items that are most critical. If some items go unaddressed, move them to the following 1:1. Let your employee know at the outset that real-time changes can be made to the agenda if a critical item emerges.

Also, to best connect with each direct report, consider that person's preferences regarding communication, collaboration, and so forth, and adjust your leadership approach accordingly. That will increase engagement and inclusion, deepen the relationship, and create trust.

End well

Clarify takeaways and action items for both parties, including how you will support next steps. When both the manager and the employee document these, chances are better that the actions will be carried out. It also builds continuity between meetings and allows for needed follow-up. After Bill implemented this change, he was reminded that his 1:1s were not mere transactions to get through but, rather, represented employees' evolving stories—something to be nurtured and developed over time. Finally, show gratitude and appreciation for your direct report's time—and start and stop on schedule to demonstrate those feelings.

Improve over Time

Ideally, both parties should leave the conversation feeling valued, respected, and well-informed, with clarity about next steps on projects, solutions to problems, and the commitments that each of them has made. However, the most important metric for success is whether your employee found the meeting both valuable tactically and fulfilling personally.

To learn where you stand and to improve these meetings over time, start by asking each team member for feedback and ideas to make future 1:1s better. Or you can anonymously survey your team with three basic questions: What's going well with the 1:1s? What's not going well? Do you have ideas for improving them? Know that what works at one time for your 1:1s may not work at another time, and what is comfortable for one direct report may not be so for another. So even if you think your current pattern is successful, keep trying new things.

What Bill learned from his first survey about 1:1s was sobering. Even more than in the exit interviews, team members raised concerns about whether he really cared about their performance or growth, citing his frequent cancellation of meetings and saying that they often couldn't get a word in edgewise. But once Bill had taken their feedback to heart, the atmosphere on his team began to shift. As he committed to meeting regularly with his employees on topics of importance to them, he found that they seemed more committed to—and proficient at—their work.

Regular individual meetings with each of your team members may feel like a burden. But meeting for 30 minutes each week with one person adds up to no more than 25 hours over the course of a year. That's not too high a price to pay to bolster your team's and your company's performance; support retention and prevent you from spending just as much time (or more) recruiting and onboarding replacements; and help each of your team members grow and achieve.

Originally published in November–December 2022. Reprint R2206L

Learn When to Say No

by Bruce Tulgan

EVER SINCE COMPANIES STARTED WORKING more cross-functionally and collaboratively, exchanging top-down management for dotted-line reporting with fuzzy accountability, work has gotten more complicated. All day every day, most of us are fielding requests. The asks are formal and informal, large and small. They're not just from direct bosses and teammates but also from "internal customers" all over the organizational chart. Add to this the demands of external stakeholders, of family, friends, and acquaintances, and sometimes even of complete strangers. The requests keep coming— across tables and through Zoom screens, by phone, e-mail, and instant message.

The inflow is daunting. And now more than ever, your professional success and personal well-being depend on how you manage it. You can't say yes to everyone and everything and do all of it well. When you take on too many or the wrong things, you waste time, energy, and money and distract yourself from what's really important. Still, no one wants to anger or disappoint colleagues or other contacts—or, worse, turn down key career and life opportunities.

You must therefore learn when and how to say both no and yes. A considered no protects you. The right yes allows you to serve others, make a difference, collaborate successfully, and increase your influence. You want to gain a reputation for saying no at the right times for the right reasons and make every single yes really count.

How do you do it? Through decades of research into what makes people the most highly valued, indispensable employees at hundreds of organizations, I have uncovered a framework that I believe works. It has three parts: assess the ask, deliver a well-reasoned no, and give a yes that sets you up for success.

Assess the Ask

When making a financial investment, most of us do some due diligence—seeking out more information so that we can make a sound judgment. When you say yes or no to a request, you're deciding where to invest your personal resources, so give the choice the same careful consideration.

That starts with insisting on a well-defined ask. Sometimes the ask is sloppy, so you misunderstand: It sounds like more or less than it is, or it sends you off in the wrong direction. That's why you ought to help yourself and the asker by getting critical details about the request. You can develop a reputation for being highly responsive if you engage in this way. It doesn't mean you're agreeing to the ask. It simply signals that you're taking your counterparts' needs seriously, whether you can help or not.

You should ask questions and take notes, clarifying every aspect of the request, including the costs and benefits. Think of the intake memos that lawyers, accountants, and doctors write—documents created for their own reference to capture the particulars of each client's need. Essentially, you're helping the asker fine-tune the request into a proposal. The memo should cover the following questions:

1. What is today's date and time? (This will help you track how the project evolves.)

2. Who is the asker?

3. What is the deliverable being requested? Be specific.

4. By when does it need to be accomplished?

5. What resources will be required?

Idea in Brief

If you're like most people, you're constantly fielding requests at work. The asks are formal and informal, large and small, and from all across the organization. The inflow is so great, you can't possibly agree to everything. So it's crucial to learn when to say no and how to say both no and yes.

Tulgan, who spent decades studying what makes people the most highly valued, indispensable employees at organizations, presents a three-part framework for managing the flood of requests. First, assess each ask, systematically gathering the details that will allow you to make an informed judgment. If you do have to turn someone down, deliver

a well-reasoned no. A good no is all about timing and logic—it's in order whenever things are not allowed, cannot be done, or should not be done. Moreover, it's communicated in a way that makes the asker feel respected. If the answer is yes, make it an effective one by explaining how you think you can help, pinning down the deliverables, and laying out a focused plan for execution.

A considered no protects you. A good yes allows you to serve others, add value, and collaborate effectively. If you become skilled at conveying both, you can avoid burnout, increase your influence, and enhance your reputation.

6. Who is the source of authority on this issue, and do you have that person or group's approval?

7. What are the possible benefits?

8. What are the obvious and hidden costs?

The bigger or more complicated the ask, the more information you should gather. Sometimes honoring the request is out of the question. Or an ask appears so insignificant that an intake memo seems unnecessary—or would take longer to draft than simply completing the request. Indeed, if you tried to drill down into every microask, people might accuse you of creating ridiculous bureaucracy. And they'd have a point. But the vast majority of requests will deserve at least some further investigation before you make a call on them. You'll find that small asks can balloon into big ones or that what at first sounds impossible turns out to be much easier than you assumed.

You might see that a seemingly silly ask is actually smart, or vice versa. That's why the intake memo should become a rock-solid habit for everything except the most minor and urgent requests.

Be sure you share your list with the asker to confirm that you're on the same page. Imagine the confidence your counterparts will gain in your promises if they see you're creating a mutually approved record of what they need—and how much more readily they'll accept your judgment of yes or no.

Zane (whose name has been changed to protect confidentiality) is an extremely capable business analyst in a large consumer-electronics company. Until recently, he had a hard time saying no at work, especially to his boss and other senior leaders, because he was so determined to prove his value.

Inundated by requests, he often found himself terribly over-committed, working harder and harder, juggling competing priorities as fast as he could. He never intended to overpromise, but he was often doubling back to renegotiate delivery dates even as he accepted new requests. Soon he started dropping balls, making mistakes, and irritating colleagues. Every incoming request felt like an attack to fend off, so at least for a while, no seemed like the only answer.

Finally, Zane's manager, Aiko, intervened and asked that all requests for his time go through her. Although he temporarily lost his power to say yes or no, he learned a lot from his boss's process, and eventually, Zane took it over himself.

"We had an intake form," Zane explains. "Who is making and authorizing this request? Is this data we have or data we need to get or start capturing going forward? Do you need analysis, and is that something we can do? And what is the business objective?"

Even after answering those questions, prioritizing competing requests could often be tricky. In one instance, Zane's boss's boss tasked him with setting up a new data-capture system "as fast as possible," just as he was pulling together a report for Aiko. The latter was a two-day project. Building the new system would take about two weeks. Should he immediately focus on the biggest big shot or first get the quick win?

Another challenge for Zane was ranking competing requests from his peers against those from his two direct reports and from people elsewhere in the organization and outside it. But using the disciplined intake-memo process, Zane got better and better at comparing how urgent or important each project really was, making smart decisions, and demonstrating to everyone his true service mindset without overextending himself.

A Well-Reasoned No

A thoughtful no, delivered at the right time, can be a huge boon, saving time and trouble for everybody down the road.

A bad no, hastily decided, causes problems for everybody, especially you. Bad nos happen when you haven't properly assessed the ask; when you let decisions be driven by personal biases, including dislike of the asker or dismissals of people who don't seem important enough; or when you decline simply because you've said yes to too many other things and don't have any capacity left. Bad nos often cause you to miss out on meaningful experiences and are also more likely to get overruled, leaving hard feelings on both sides.

A good no is all about timing and logic. You should say no to things that *are not allowed, cannot be done,* or that, on balance, *should not be done.* I call these the "no gates," a concept I borrowed from a project management technique called stage-gate reviews, which divide initiatives into distinct phases and then subject each to a "go, no go" decision.

The first gate is the easiest to understand. If there are procedures, guidelines, or regulations that prohibit you from doing something—or someone has already made it clear that this category of work is off-limits to you, at least for now—then you simply give a straight no. (If you think it's against the rules for everybody, please also consider talking the requester out of pursuing the idea.)

What do you say? "I don't have discretion here. This request violates policy/rules/law. So you really shouldn't make it at all. Perhaps I can help you reframe your request within the rules so that it can then be considered."

Turning people down at the second gate is also straightforward (at least sometimes). If the request isn't feasible, you say, "I simply can't do it." If you just don't have the ability to deliver on it, then you say, "Sorry, that's outside my skill set. I'm not even close."

What if you don't currently have the experience and skills to handle the request quickly and confidently—but you could acquire them? The answer still might be no. But the answer could also be "This is not my specialty. That said, if you accept that I'd need extra time to climb a learning curve, then I'll take a crack at it." It could be a development opportunity for you and, in the end, give the requester a new go-to person (you) on this sort of project.

The most common reason for "I cannot," however, is overcommitment. In those instances, people tend to say things like "With all the other priorities I'm balancing, I don't have the availability to do it anytime soon." That's a forced no. If you can't avoid it, try to preserve the opportunity to fulfill the request later or else help out down the road when you are available.

What's the best way to respond? "I'm already committed to other responsibilities and projects. I'd love to do this for you at a later time. If that's not possible, I'd love to be of service somehow in the future."

The third gate is the trickiest because whether something merits doing isn't always clear at first. You need to make a judgment on the likelihood of your success, on the potential return on investment, and on the fit with your and your organization's priorities. And sometimes the answer to the request is "maybe" or "not yet."

What do you say in those cases? "I need to know more. Let me ask you the following questions. . . ." Essentially, you're getting the person in need of help to make a more thorough or convincing proposal.

What if you do understand the ask and you don't think it's a worthwhile goal for you right now? You might say, "That's not something I should say yes to at this time because the likelihood of success is low," ". . . the necessary resources are too great," ". . . it's not in alignment with the current priorities," or ". . . the likely outcome is [otherwise somehow not desirable]."

When it comes to timing, the most important thing is to thoroughly engage with the request. Then answer quickly. Don't give a precipitous no, or you'll risk seeming dismissive. But don't string your counterpart along, either. If your no really means "not at the moment but soon," then let the person know that. If the answer is "No, but I know somebody who can" or "No, but I can provide you with aid that will help somebody else do it," then say that as soon as possible. If the answer is "I may not, cannot, or should not do it, and it is a bad idea, so you shouldn't do it either," have that conversation before the asker presses you or someone else further.

Once Zane routinely began tuning in to every ask and doing his due diligence, he found it much easier to see when he should decline a request and became far more confident delivering a well-reasoned no—or a "not yet." For example, around the time that he was balancing that report for Aiko with setting up the new system for her boss, Zane had to decline or delay filling several other requests. As usual, he gave many standard "That data is simply not in the system" responses. But he also said no to a request for a wild-goose chase from a peer of his boss who had a history of wasting his time. "I wasn't building a correlation model *again* to once again *not* find the pattern he was looking for," Zane explains, noting that he also gave Aiko a heads-up to make sure nobody would be surprised. He also delayed completing a request from another executive peer of Aiko's, saying something along the lines of "We've never collected that particular data before. Maybe we can start, but I wouldn't be free to work on that for a few weeks."

Because of Zane's increasingly thorough, businesslike approach, his colleagues came to deeply value his assessments and responses and—over time—his judgment.

An Effective Yes

Every good no makes room for a better yes—one that adds value, builds relationships, and enhances your reputation.

What is a better yes?

It's aligned with the mission, values, priorities, ground rules, and marching orders from above. It's for something that you can do, ideally well, fast, and with confidence. In other words, it involves one of your specialties—or an opportunity to build a new one. It allows you to make an investment of time, energy, and resources in something that has a high likelihood of success and offers significant potential benefits.

The key to a great yes is clear communication and a focused plan for execution. First, explain exactly why you're saying yes: You can enrich the project, you want to collaborate, you see the benefits. Then pin down your plan of action, especially for a deliverable of any scope.

Make sure you agree on the details, including what the requester needs from you, what you will do together, how and when the work will be done, who has oversight, and when you'll discuss the issue next. If this is a multistep process, you might need to have several of those conversations as you go along.

As his reputation for professionalism and good judgment grew, Zane was in greater demand but also had more and more discretion to choose among competing responsibilities and projects. As the company moved toward a more sophisticated approach to business intelligence (data collection, analysis, reporting, and modeling for prediction), his input was sought by a number of executives he had worked with, and his opinion was given a lot of weight. As a result, Zane was made the lead analyst on the new enterprise-resource-management system implementation, which he describes as "the greatest professional development experience" of his career.

Most people have too much to do and too little time. Saying yes to requests from bosses, teammates, and others can make you feel important but can be a prescription for burnout.

The only way to be sustainably successful is to get really good at saying no in a way that makes people feel respected and to say yes only when your reasoning is sound and you have a clear plan of attack.

Originally published in September–October 2020. Reprint R2005M

Begin with Trust

by Frances Frei and Anne Morriss

ON A SPRING AFTERNOON IN 2017, Travis Kalanick, then the CEO of
Uber, walked into a conference room at the company's Bay Area headquarters. One of us, Frances, was waiting for him. Meghan Joyce, the
company's general manager for the United States and Canada, had
reached out to us, hoping that we could guide the company as it
sought to heal from a series of deep, self-inflicted wounds. We had
a track record of helping organizations, many of them founder-led,
tackle messy leadership and culture challenges.

We were skeptical about Uber. Everything we'd read about the
company suggested it had little hope of redemption. At the time,
the company was an astonishingly disruptive and successful start-up,
but its success seemed to have come at the price of basic decency. In
early 2017, for example, when taxi drivers went on strike in New York
City to protest President Trump's travel ban, Uber appeared to have
used tactics to profit from the situation—a move that prompted
widespread outrage and a #deleteUber campaign. A month later, not
long before the meeting, an Uber engineer named Susan Fowler had
blogged courageously about her experiences of harassment and discrimination at the company, which caused more outrage. Footage of
Kalanick had then emerged, in a video that went viral, of his interaction with an Uber driver, where he appeared dismissive of the pain
of earning a living in a post-Uber world. Additional charges leveled
at the company in this period reinforced Uber's reputation as a cold-
blooded operator that would do almost anything to win.

Despite our skepticism, Frances had gone to California to hear
Kalanick out. (Anne was building her own company at the time, so

she took a back seat on the project.) As Frances waited for him to make his entrance, she braced herself for the smug CEO she'd read about. But that wasn't who walked in. Kalanick arrived humbled and introspective. He had thought a lot about how the cultural values he'd instilled in the company—the very values that had fueled Uber's success—had also been misused and distorted on his watch. He expressed deep respect for what his team had achieved but also acknowledged that he'd put some people in leadership roles without giving them the training or mentorship to be effective. Whatever mistakes Kalanick had made up to that point, he revealed a sincere desire to do the right thing as a leader.

We regrouped back in Cambridge, Massachusetts, and debated whether to take on the project. There were lots of reasons to stay far away from it. The work would be hard and its outcome uncertain, to say nothing of the brutal commute. Uber's workforce was frustrated, and the brand was becoming toxic. But we realized that if we could help get Uber back on the right path, then we could offer a road map to countless others trying to restore humanity to organizations that had lost their way. So we signed on.

After making that decision, we knew exactly where to start. With trust.

Empowerment Leadership

We think of trust as precious, and yet it's the basis for almost everything we do as civilized people. Trust is the reason we're willing to exchange our hard-earned paychecks for goods and services, pledge our lives to another person in marriage, cast a ballot for someone who will represent our interests. We rely on laws and contracts as safety nets, but even they are ultimately built on trust in the institutions that enforce them. We don't know that justice will be served if something goes wrong, but we have enough faith in the system that we're willing to make high-stakes deals with relative strangers.

Trust is also one of the most essential forms of capital a leader has. Building trust, however, often requires thinking about leadership from a new perspective. The traditional leadership narrative

Idea in Brief

The Starting Point

The traditional leadership narrative is all about you: your talents, charisma, and moments of courage and instinct. But real leadership is about your people and creating the conditions for them to fully realize their own capacity and power. To do this, you have to develop stores of trust.

The Challenge

How do leaders build trust? By focusing on its core drivers: authenticity, logic, and empathy.

People tend to trust you when they think they're interacting with the real you, when they have faith in your judgment and competence, and when they believe you care about them.

The Way Forward

When leaders have trouble with trust, it's usually because they're weak on one of those three drivers. To develop or restore trust, identify which driver you're "wobbly" on, and then work on strengthening it.

is all about you: your vision and strategy; your ability to make the tough calls and rally the troops; your talents, your charisma, your heroic moments of courage and instinct. But leadership really isn't about you. It's about empowering other people as a result of your presence, and about making sure that the impact of your leadership continues into your absence.

That's the fundamental principle we've learned in the course of dedicating our careers to making leaders and organizations better. Your job as a leader is to create the conditions for your people to fully realize their own capacity and power. And that's true not only when you're in the trenches with them but also when you're not around and even—this is the cleanest test—when you've permanently moved on from the team. We call it empowerment leadership. The more trust you build, the more possible it is to practice this kind of leadership.

The Core Drivers of Trust

So how do you build up stores of this foundational leadership capital? In our experience, trust has three core drivers: authenticity, logic, and empathy. People tend to trust you when they believe they are interacting with the real you (authenticity), when they have faith in your judgment and competence (logic), and when they feel that you care about them (empathy). When trust is lost, it can almost always be traced back to a breakdown in one of these three drivers.

People don't always realize how the information (or more often, the misinformation) that they're broadcasting may undermine their own trustworthiness. What's worse, stress tends to amplify the problem, causing people to double down on behaviors that make others skeptical. For example, they might unconsciously mask their true selves in a job interview, even though that's precisely the type of less-than-fully-authentic behavior that reduces their chance of being hired.

The good news is that most of us generate a stable pattern of trust signals, which means a small change in behavior can go a long way. In moments when trust is broken, or fails to get any real traction, it's usually the same driver that has gone wobbly on us—authenticity, empathy, or logic. We call this driver your "trust wobble." In simple terms, it's the driver that's most likely to fail you.

Everybody, it turns out, has a trust wobble. To build trust as a leader, you first need to figure out what yours is.

Build It, and They Will Come

To identify your wobble, think of a recent moment when you were not trusted as much as you wanted to be. Maybe you lost an important sale or didn't get a stretch assignment. Maybe someone simply doubted your ability to execute. With that moment in mind, do something hard: Give the other person in your story the benefit of the doubt. Let's call that person your "skeptic." Assume that your skeptic's reservations were valid and that you were the one responsible for the breakdown in trust. This exercise only works if you own it.

If you had to choose from our three trust drivers, which would you say went wobbly on you in this situation? Did your skeptic feel you were misrepresenting some part of yourself or your story? If so, that's an authenticity problem. Did your skeptic feel you might be

The trust triangle

Trust has three drivers: authenticity, logic, and empathy. When trust is lost, it can almost always be traced back to a breakdown in one of them. To build trust as a leader, you first need to figure out which driver you "wobble" on.

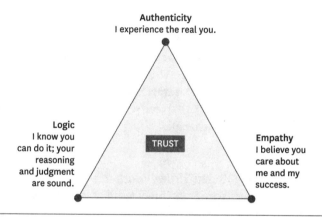

Authenticity
I experience the real you.

Logic
I know you can do it; your reasoning and judgment are sound.

TRUST

Empathy
I believe you care about me and my success.

putting your own interests first? If so, that's an empathy problem. Did your skeptic question the rigor of your analysis or your ability to execute on an ambitious plan? If so, that's a logic problem.

Now stand back and try to look at your pattern of wobbles across multiple incidents. Pick three or four interactions that stand out to you, for whatever reason, and do a quick trust diagnostic for each one. What does your typical wobble seem to be? Does the pattern change under stress or with different kinds of stakeholders? For example, do you wobble on one trait with your direct reports but on a different one with people who have authority over you? That's not uncommon.

This exercise works best if you bring at least one person along for your diagnostic ride, ideally someone who knows you well. Sharing your analysis can be clarifying—even liberating—and will help you test and refine your hypothesis. In our experience, about 20% of self-assessments need a round of revision, so choose a partner who can keep you honest. Consider going back and testing your analysis directly by speaking openly about it with your skeptic. This conversation alone can be a powerful way to rebuild trust. When you take responsibility for a wobble, you reveal your humanity (authenticity) and analytic chops (logic) while communicating your commitment to the relationship (empathy).

Overcoming Your Wobble

Over the past decade we've helped all kinds of leaders—from seasoned politicians to Millennial entrepreneurs to the heads of multibillion-dollar companies—wrestle with trust issues. In doing so, we've learned a lot about strategies you can deploy to overcome your own trust wobbles. Let's explore what's most effective for each of the drivers in our trust triangle.

Empathy

Most high-achieving leaders struggle with this one. Signaling a lack of empathy is a major barrier to empowerment leadership. If people think you care more about yourself than about others, they won't trust you enough to lead them.

Empathy wobbles are common among people who are analytical and driven to learn. They often get impatient with those who aren't similarly motivated or who take longer than they do to understand something. Additionally, the tools and experience of the modern workplace continually distract or prevent us from demonstrating empathy, by imposing 24-hour demands on our time and putting at our disposal all sorts of technologies that compete for our attention at any given moment. Our beeping and buzzing devices constantly assert our self-importance, sometimes smack in the middle of interactions with the very people we're working to empower and lead.

We advise empathy wobblers to pay close attention to their behavior in group settings, particularly when other people have the floor. Consider what often happens in a meeting: When it kicks off, most people feel very engaged. But as soon as empathy wobblers understand the concepts under discussion and have contributed their ideas, they lose interest. Their engagement plummets and remains low until the gathering (mercifully) comes to an end. Instead of paying attention, they often multitask, check their phones, engage in flamboyant displays of boredom—anything to make clear that this meeting is beneath them. Unfortunately, the cost of these indulgences is trust. If you signal that you matter more than everyone else, why should anyone trust the direction you're going in? What's in it for the rest of us to come along?

There's a basic solution to this problem. Instead of focusing on what you need in that meeting, work to ensure that everyone else gets what they need. Take radical responsibility for the others in the room. Share the burden of moving the dialogue forward, even if it's not your meeting. Search for the resonant examples that will bring the concepts to life, and don't disengage until everyone else in the room understands. This is almost impossible to do if texting or checking email is an option, so put away your devices. Everyone knows you're not taking notes on their good ideas.

Indeed, the last thing we'll say on empathy is this: If you do nothing else to change your behavior, put away your phone more frequently. Put it truly away, out of sight and out of reach, not just flipped over for a few minutes at a time. You'll be amazed at the change in the quality of your interactions and your ability to build trust.

Logic

If people don't always have confidence in the rigor of your ideas, or if they don't have full faith in your ability to deliver on them, then logic is probably your wobble. If they don't trust your judgment, why would they want you at the wheel?

When logic is the problem, we advise going back to the data. Root the case you're making in sound evidence, speak about the things you know to be true beyond a reasonable doubt, and then—this is the hard part—stop there. One reason Larry Bird was such an extraordinary basketball player was that he only took shots he knew he could reliably make. That choice made him different from other great players who let ego and adrenaline cloud their shooting judgment. Bird studied and practiced so relentlessly that by the time the ball left his hands in the heat of competition, he knew exactly where it was going. If logic is your wobble, take Bird's example and learn to "play within yourself."

Once you get comfortable with how that feels, start expanding what you know. Along the way, make an effort to learn from other people. Their insight is among your most valuable resources, but to access it, you must be willing to reveal that you don't have all the answers—something leaders often resist. Engaging people about their experience has the additional benefit of communicating who you are and what energizes you professionally—an authenticity boost.

For most logic wobblers, however, rigor isn't the issue. Much of the time, the problem is the perception of wobbly logic rather than the reality of it. Why does this happen? Because they're not communicating their ideas effectively.

There are generally two ways to communicate complex thoughts. The first takes your audience on a journey, with twists and turns and context and dramatic tension, until they eventually get to the payoff. Many of the world's best storytellers use this technique. You can visualize this approach by imagining an inverted triangle. The journeying storyteller starts at the top, at the inverted base of the triangle, and traces an enchantingly meandering route down to its point.

If logic is your wobble, however, that's a risky path to take. With all that circuitous journeying, you're likely to lose your audience along the way rather than build trust in your judgment. Listeners may even abandon you at one of your narrative turns.

To avoid that, try flipping the imaginary triangle upright. Start with your main point, or headline, at the top of the triangle, and then work your way down, building a base of reinforcing evidence. This approach signals a clarity of vision and a full command of the facts. Everyone has a much better chance of following your logic. Even if you get interrupted along the way, you'll at least have had a chance to communicate your key idea.

Authenticity

If people feel they're not getting access to the "real" you—to a full and complete accounting of what you know, think, and feel—then you probably have an authenticity wobble.

A quick test: How different is your professional persona from the one that shows up around family and friends? If there's a sharp difference, what are you getting in return for masking or minimizing certain parts of yourself? What's the payoff? Being your "real self" sounds nice in theory, but there can be powerful reasons for holding back certain truths. The calculation can be highly practical at times, if wrenching—as in deciding to stay closeted in a workplace that's hostile to queer identities. There may also be times when expressing your authentic feelings may risk harmful consequences: Women, for example, are disproportionately penalized for displaying negative emotions in the workplace, and Black men are burdened by the false stereotype that they are predisposed to anger. We're not talking here about moments of prudent self-censorship, which sometimes can't be divorced from a larger context of bias or low psychological safety. Instead, we're talking about inauthenticity as a strategy, a way of navigating the workplace. If this is how you operate, you're dealing with an authenticity wobble.

In our experience, although withholding your true self may sometimes help you solve problems in the short term, it puts an artificial cap on trust and, by extension, on your ability to lead. When people sense that you're concealing the truth or being less than authentic, they're far less willing to make themselves vulnerable to you in the ways that leadership demands.

We've observed the cost of inauthenticity up close in the performance of diverse teams. Diversity can be a tremendous asset in today's marketplace, and the companies that get it right often enjoy powerful competitive tailwinds. But this advantage isn't automatic. Simply populating your team with diverse perspectives and experiences doesn't always translate into better performance. In fact, the uncomfortable truth is that diverse teams can underperform homogenous teams if they're not managed actively for differences among members. That is due in part to a phenomenon called the common information effect, which works like this: As human beings, we tend to focus on the things we have in common with other people. We tend to seek out and affirm our shared knowledge, because it confirms our value and kinship with the group. Diverse teams, by definition, have less common information readily available to them to use in collective decision-making.

Consider two teams of three people, one in which the three members are different from one another, and the other in which they're similar. If both teams are managed in exactly the same way—if they simply follow the same best practices in group facilitation, for example—the homogenous team is likely to perform better. No amount of feedback or number of trust falls can overcome the strength of the common information effect.

But the effect only holds if people wobble on authenticity. When they choose to bring their unique selves to the table—that is, the parts of themselves that are different from other people—they can create an unbeatable advantage by expanding the amount of information the team can access. The result is an inclusive team that's likely to outperform (by a long shot) both homogenous teams and diverse teams that aren't actively managed for inclusion. (See the exhibit "Trust, diversity, and team performance.")

This expansion of knowledge and its obvious benefits rely on the courage of authenticity wobblers. We know how difficult sharing who we really are can be, and we also know that it's sometimes too much to ask. But if we regularly give in to the pressure to hold back our unique selves, then we suppress the most valuable parts of ourselves. Not only do we end up concealing the very thing the world needs most from us—our differences—but we also make it harder for people to trust us as leaders.

Here's the reason to care, even if you don't see yourself as different: All of us pay the price of inauthentic interactions, and all of us have a better chance of thriving in inclusive environments where authenticity can flourish. Gender bias, in other words, is not just a woman's problem. Systemic racism is not just an African American or Latinx problem. It's our shared moral and organizational imperative to create workplaces where the burdens of being different are shouldered by all of us. After all, we will all benefit wildly from eliminating them.

Trust, diversity, and team performance

Diversity doesn't automatically confer advantages in decision-making. In fact, if diverse teams aren't managed actively for inclusion, they can underperform homogenous ones. That's because shared knowledge is key in decision-making, and diverse teams, by definition, start out with less of it. But if you create conditions of trust that allow diverse team members to bring their unique perspectives and experiences to the table, you can expand the amount of knowledge your team can access—and create an unbeatable advantage.

Diverse teams
A diverse store
of knowledge is
partly shared.

Homogenous teams
A common store
of knowledge is
fully shared.

Inclusive teams
A diverse store
of knowledge is
fully shared.

One of the lessons we've learned in our work with organizations is that creating spaces where authenticity can thrive is not as hard as it may seem. It is an urgent, achievable goal that requires far less audacity than disrupting industries or growing complex organizations—things leaders do every day with deep conviction in the outcomes. If all of us take responsibility for creating companies where difference can thrive, and all of us take responsibility for showing up in them authentically, then our chances of achieving true inclusion—and building high levels of trust—start to look pretty good.

So pay less attention to what you think people want to hear and more attention to what you need to say to them. Reveal your full humanity to the world, regardless of what your critics say. And while you're at it, take exquisite care of people who are different from you, confident in the knowledge that their difference is the very thing that could unleash your potential and your organization's.

In Myself I Trust

We've argued that the foundation of empowerment leadership is getting other people to trust you. That's certainly true, but there's one last thing you need to know. The path to empowerment leadership doesn't begin when other people start to trust you. It begins when you start to trust yourself.

To be a truly empowering leader, you need to take stock of where you wobble not only in your relationships with others but also in your relationship with yourself. Are you being honest with yourself about your ambitions, or are you ignoring what really excites and inspires you? If you're hiding something from yourself, you've got an authenticity problem you need to address. Do you acknowledge your own needs and attend properly to them? If not, you've got to adopt a more empathetic posture toward yourself. Do you lack conviction in your own ideas and ability to perform? If so, you've got some logic issues to work out.

Doing this work is important as a leader, for an arguably obvious reason. If you don't trust yourself, why should anybody else trust you?

A Campaign to Rebuild Trust

Let's now return to Uber. When we began working with the company, it was certainly wobbling—so much so that we diagnosed it as "a hot mess."

What was going on?

Consider the basic trust-related facts. There's no question that Uber had empathy problems. The company's focus on growth at all costs meant that relationships with stakeholders, particularly drivers and employees, needed real attention. Riders also needed to be assured that their safety wouldn't come second to the company's financial performance. Additionally, despite its disruptive success, Uber hadn't answered questions about the long-term viability of its business model or about whether its managers had the skills to lead an organization of its expansive scale and scope. These were unaddressed logic problems. Finally, the company's war-room mentality was undermining its authenticity. In the "us versus them" culture at Uber, people were skeptical that they were getting the full story.

By the time Frances began working with Kalanick, he had already begun making changes to steady the company's trust wobbles. He had hired Eric Holder, for example, who had served as U.S. attorney general under President Obama, to lead a rigorous internal investigation into harassment and discrimination—and when Holder made a sweeping set of recommendations, Kalanick took action to implement them. The company was also on the verge of rolling out new driver-tipping functionality, which would go on to generate $600 million in additional driver compensation in the first year of its launch. New safety features were in development, too, designed to give both drivers and riders additional tools to protect themselves.

Kalanick didn't get the chance to see most of these initiatives to completion, at least not from the CEO chair. In June 2017, he was forced out as CEO, although he retained his board seat and an equity stake in the company until December 2019, when he gave both up. He was ultimately replaced by Dara Khosrowshahi, the former Expedia CEO, who had a track record of effective leadership at the helm of young companies.

Frances soon began working with Khosrowshahi to continue the campaign to rebuild trust internally. Together they led an effort to rewrite the company's cultural values, one that invited input from all 15,000 employees on the principles that they wanted Uber to live by. The new motto they settled on was "We do the right thing. Period." Other early trust wins for Khosrowshahi included strengthening relationships with regulators and executing a logic-driven focus on the services and markets that were most defensible.

Most of the work we did during this period was aimed at rebuilding trust at the employee level. Some things were easy to identify and fix, like ratcheting down the widespread, empathy-pulverizing practice of texting during meetings about the other people in the meeting, a tech-company norm that shocked us when we first experienced it. We introduced a new norm of turning off all personal technology and putting it away during meetings, which forced people to start making eye contact with their colleagues again.

Other challenges were harder to tackle, like the need to upskill thousands of managers. Our take was that Uber had underinvested in its people during its period of hypergrowth, leaving many managers unprepared for the increasing complexity of their jobs. We addressed this logic wobble with a massive infusion of executive education, using a virtual classroom to engage employees in live case discussions—our pedagogy of choice—whether they were in San Francisco, London, or Hyderabad. Although our pilot program was voluntary and classes were sometimes scheduled at absurdly inconvenient times, 6,000 Uber employees based in more than 50 countries each participated in 24 hours of instruction over the course of 60 days. It was an extraordinary pace, scale, and absorption of management education.

The curriculum gave people tools and concepts to develop quickly as leaders while flipping a whole lot of upside-down communication triangles. Employees gained the skills not only to listen better but also to talk in ways that made it easier to collaborate across business units and geographies. Frances went out in the field, visiting key global offices in her first 30 days on the job, carving out protected spaces to listen to employees and communicate leadership's commitment to building a company worthy of its people. At a time when many employees were conflicted about their Uber affiliations, Frances made it a point to wear an Uber T-shirt every day until the entire company was proud to be on the payroll.

Within a year, Uber was less wobbly. There were still problems to be solved, but indicators such as employee sentiment, brand health, and driver compensation were all heading in the right direction, and the march toward an IPO began in earnest. Good people were deciding to stay with the company, more good people were joining, and, in what had become our favorite indicator of progress, an increasing number of Uber T-shirts could now be spotted on city streets. It was all a testament to the talent, creativity, and commitment to learning at every level of the organization—and to the new foundation of trust that Kalanick and Khosrowshahi had been able to build.

Originally published in May–June 2020. **Reprint** R2003H

About the Contributors

ERIC M. ANICICH is an assistant professor of management and organization at the University of Southern California Marshall School of Business. His research focuses on the forms and functions of social hierarchy within groups.

SUSAN (SUE) J. ASHFORD is an award-winning scholar and the author of *The Power of Flexing: How to Use Small Daily Experiments to Create Big Life-Changing Growth*. She is the Michael and Susan Jandernoa Professor of Management and Organizations at the Ross School of Business, University of Michigan.

JAMES DETERT is the author of *Choosing Courage* (Harvard Business Review Press, 2021) and the John L. Colley Professor of Business Administration at the University of Virginia's Darden School of Business.

FRANCES FREI is the UPS Foundation Professor of Service Management at Harvard Business School and a coauthor of *Unleashed: The Unapologetic Leader's Guide to Empowering Everyone Around You* (Harvard Business Review Press, 2020) and *Move Fast and Fix Things: The Trusted Leader's Guide to Solving Hard Problems and Accelerating Change* (Harvard Business Review Press, 2023).

JOHN J. GABARRO was the UPS Foundation Professor of Human Resource Management, Emeritus, at Harvard Business School. He was the author or coauthor of five books, including *Interpersonal Behavior* (with Anthony G. Athos) and *The Dynamics of Taking Charge*, which won the 1988 New Directions in Leadership Award.

DIANE GHERSON is the former chief human resources officer of IBM and a senior lecturer of business administration at Harvard Business School.

LYNDA GRATTON is a professor of management practice at London Business School and the founder of HSM Advisory, a future-of-work research consultancy. Her most recent book is *Redesigning Work: How to Transform Your Organization and Make Hybrid Work for Everyone*.

167

MARTINE HAAS is the Lauder Chair Professor of Management at The Wharton School and Director of the Lauder Institute for Management and International Studies at the University of Pennsylvania. Her research focuses on collaboration and teamwork in global organizations.

JACOB B. HIRSH is an assistant professor of organizational behavior and human resource management at the University of Toronto. His research explores the cognitive and affective dynamics of personality, motivation, and decision-making.

REBECCA HOMKES is a lecturer at the London Business School's Department of Strategy and Entrepreneurship, a faculty member at Duke Corporate Executive Education, and a former fellow at the London School of Economics' Centre for Economic Performance. A high-growth-strategy specialist, her book on breakthrough growth during uncertainty, *Survive Reset Thrive*, will be published in late 2023.

QUY NGUYEN HUY is the Solvay Chaired Professor of Technological Innovation at INSEAD and Academic Director of the INSEAD China Initiative.

HERMINIA IBARRA is the Charles Handy Professor of Organizational Behavior at London Business School and the author of *Working Identity* and *Act Like a Leader, Think Like a Leader* (both Harvard Business Review Press, new editions forthcoming).

ZAHIRA JASER is an assistant professor at the University of Sussex Business School and Deputy Director of the MBA program. Her work focuses on how managers bridge multilevel relationships in organizations and how hierarchies can be made more fluid. She is the editor of *The Connecting Leader: Serving Concurrently as a Leader and a Follower*. For updates follow Zahira on LinkedIn or on Twitter @ZahiraJaser.

JOHN P. KOTTER is a bestselling author, award-winning business and management thought leader, business entrepreneur, and the

Konosuke Matsushita Professor of Leadership, Emeritus, at Harvard Business School. His ideas, books, and company, Kotter, help people lead organizations in an era of increasingly rapid change. He is a co-author of *Change*, which details how leaders can leverage challenges and opportunities to make sustainable workplace changes in a rapidly accelerating world.

SKY MIHAYLO is an equity-driven policy strategist. Formerly a Policy and Research fellow at the Center for WorkLife Law, they worked closely with founder Joan C. Williams on gender and racial bias research and developing Bias Interrupters. They hold a master of public policy degree from the University of California, Berkeley, and currently work as a Government Innovation fellow at the Harvard Kennedy School Government Performance Lab (GPL).

ANNE MORRISS is an entrepreneur and the executive founder of the Leadership Consortium. She is also the coauthor of *Unleashed: The Unapologetic Leader's Guide to Empowering Everyone Around You* (Harvard Business Review Press, 2020) and *Move Fast and Fix Things: The Trusted Leader's Guide to Solving Hard Problems and Accelerating Change* (Harvard Business Review Press, 2023).

MARK MORTENSEN is an associate professor and former Area Chair of Organizational Behavior at INSEAD. His research focuses on teams and collaboration, the changing nature of work, and the employee value proposition.

STEVEN G. ROGELBERG holds the title of Chancellor's Professor at the University of North Carolina Charlotte for his distinguished national, international, and interdisciplinary contributions. He is the author of *Glad We Met: The Art and Science of 1:1 Meetings* and *The Surprising Science of Meetings: How You Can Lead Your Team to Peak Performance*. He writes and speaks about leadership, teams, meetings, and engagement. Follow him on LinkedIn or find more information at stevenrogelberg.com.

ANNE SCOULAR is a cofounder of Meyler Campbell, which trains senior leaders to coach. She is also an associate scholar at the University of Oxford's Saïd Business School and the author of *The Financial Times Guide to Business Coaching.*

DINA DENHAM SMITH is an executive coach to senior leaders at world-leading brands such as Adobe, Netflix, PwC, Dropbox, Stripe, and numerous other high-growth companies. A former business executive herself, she is the founder and CEO of Cognitas and helps leaders and their teams reach new heights of success. Connect with her on LinkedIn.

CHARLES (CHARLIE) SULL is a cofounder of CultureX, where he advises C-suite leaders of top-level organizations on the most effective ways to build robust cultures that achieve strategic objectives. He helped develop the underlying AI platform at MIT that powers the CultureX platform and related research, which has reached an audience of millions and been featured in the *New York Times, Wall Street Journal,* and Brené Brown's podcast, *Dare to Lead with Brené Brown.*

DONALD SULL is a senior lecturer at the MIT Sloan School of Management and cofounder of CultureX.

BRUCE TULGAN is the founder of the management research, training, and consulting firm, RainmakerThinking, and the author of numerous books, including *The Art of Being Indispensable at Work* (Harvard Business Review Press, 2020).

JOAN C. WILLIAMS is a Sullivan Professor of Law at University of California Law, San Francisco, and the founding director of the Center for WorkLife Law. An expert on social inequality, she is the author of twelve books, including *Bias Interrupted: Creating Inclusion for Real and for Good* (Harvard Business Review Press, 2021) and *White Working Class: Overcoming Class Cluelessness in America* (Harvard Business Review Press, 2019). To learn about her evidence-based, metrics-driven approach to eradicating implicit bias in the workplace, visit www.biasinterrupters.org.

Index

expectations
mutual, 46, 56–57
vertical code-switching and, 6–7

fairness, 40
in hybrid workplaces, 99–104
fallibility, 47–48
fear, of change, 28, 37–40
Fearn, Mark, 129
feedback
coaching and, 123, 133
at IBM, 11
manager skill in, 8, 9, 11
one-on-one meetings and,
137–139, 140, 142, 143–144
Figley, C.R., 39
flexibility, 40, 111, 143
flexible work, 4–5, 99–104
followership skills, 25
4-D teams, 78–85
framing, 65–68
Frei, Frances, 153–166

Gabarro, John J., 43–59
GapJumpers, 93
General Mills, 81–82
geographic diversity
challenges for teams from, 80–82,
83–84
incomplete information sharing
and, 83–84
Gherson, Diane, 1–15
Gibbons, Frank, 43–47
Glassdoor, 14
goals
coaching and, 125
execution and, 107–109
knowing your boss's, 48–51
tailoring your pitch for, 63–65
team effectiveness and, 77, 78–79

Goleman, Daniel, 121
Google, 91
Grant, Adam, 69
gratitude, 143
Gratton, Lynda, 1–15
GROW model, 124–128
growth, managers in, 6–9
growth mindset, 130

Haas, Martine, 77–87, 99–104
Hackman, J. Richard, 77, 82, 85
Hewlett-Packard, Santa Rosa
Systems, 35
hierarchies, 119
manager roles in, 2
at Telstra, 12
hiring
bias in, 90–92
hybrid workplaces and, 104
interviews for, 91–92
referrals in, 91
Hirsh, Jacob B., 6–7
Holder, Eric, 165
Homkes, Rebecca, 105–118
honesty, 46, 58
housework, office, 92, 94
human resources (HR)
administrative work and, 10
execution and, 114–116
humility, 21
Huy, Quy Nguyen, 27–42
hybridity competence, 101–102
hybridity configuration, 102–104
hybridity positioning, 99–100
hybrid workplaces, 99–104
managing, 102–104
power and, 99–102

Ibarra, Herminia, 7, 119–134
IBM, 9–11, 14, 15

Engage with HBR content the way you want, on any device.

With HBR's subscription plans, you can access world-renowned case studies from Harvard Business School and receive four **free eBooks**. Download and customize prebuilt **slide decks and graphics** from our **Data & Visuals** collection. With HBR's archive, top 50 best-selling articles, and five new articles every day, HBR is more than just a magazine.

Subscribe Today
HBR.org/success

The most important management ideas all in one place.

We hope you enjoyed this book from *Harvard Business Review*. Now you can get even more with HBR's 10 Must Reads Boxed Set. From books on leadership and strategy to managing yourself and others, this 6-book collection delivers articles on the most essential business topics to help you succeed.

HBR's 10 Must Reads Series

The definitive collection of ideas and best practices on our most sought-after topics from the best minds in business.

- Change Management
- Collaboration
- Communication
- Emotional Intelligence
- Innovation
- Leadership
- Making Smart Decisions
- Managing Across Cultures
- Managing People
- Managing Yourself
- Strategic Marketing
- Strategy
- Teams
- The Essentials

hbr.org/mustreads

Buy for your team, clients, or event.
Visit hbr.org/bulksales for quantity discount rates.